Half-Baked Gourmet™

PARTLY HOMEMADE TOTALLY DELICIOUS

PARTY FOOD

200 Quick-and-Easy Recipes • *Jan Turner Hazard*

A ROUNDTABLE PRESS BOOK

HPBOOKS

Most HPBooks are available at special quantity discounts for bulk purchases for sales promotions, premiums, fund-raising, or educational use. Special books, or book excerpts, can also be created to fit specific needs.

For details, write: Special Markets, The Berkley Publishing Group, 375 Hudson Street, New York, NY 10014.

HPBooks
Published by The Berkley Publishing Group
A division of Penguin Group (USA) Inc.
375 Hudson Street
New York, New York 10014

Copyright © 2004 Roundtable Press, Inc.
Design: Charles Kreloff
Illustrations: Tony Persiani
Cover photograph © Foodpix/Mark Thomas

Roundtable Press, Inc.
Directors: Julie Merberg, Marsha Melnick
Executive Editor: Patty Brown
Editor: Sara Newberry
Production Editor: John Glenn
www.roundtablepressinc.com

First edition: September 2004

This book has been cataloged with the Library of Congress.
ISBN 1-55788-441-2
Printed and bound in China

10 9 8 7 6 5 4 3 2 1

Contents

When it comes to entertaining, most people don't have the time to shop for and prepare labor-intensive dishes, and most hosts prefer to be enjoying the pleasure of their guests' company rather than slaving away in the kitchen. Throwing a party shouldn't be a chore—parties should be fun for everyone, including the host.

As you peruse this book, you will see that I have found ways to take the work out of party-giving by using prepared ingredients such as prebaked mini phyllo dough shells, bottled salsas and sauces, and flavored cream cheeses that will help to keep your preparation, cooking, and clean-up time to a minimum. I have also cut down on shopping time by using fewer ingredients, so you can breeze in and out of the supermarket. Many of these items can be kept on hand in your pantry, fridge, or freezer, just waiting for your next spontaneous soirée!

Whether you're preparing cocktails for a crowd or finger foods for just a few friends, you'll never be at a loss for what to serve your guests with help from **Half-Baked Gourmet: Party Foods.**

A WORD ABOUT THE INGREDIENTS

When you use fewer ingredients, each one of them should be of the highest quality available. If you have trouble deciding which brand to buy, err on the side of quality and choose one with all-natural ingredients.

If you have difficulty locating a particular ingredient at your supermarket, remember that many products are available at specialty stores or online.

SALSAS, SAUCES, AND CONDIMENTS

There are hundreds of jarred **salsas** on super-market shelves and in the refrigerated case. The heat levels, starting with the least spicy, are usually labeled mild, medium and hot. Use the salsa brand that has the flavor that you like, at whatever heat level you enjoy. I found Green Mountain® salsas to have a good consistency. Frontera® salsas are delicately fire-roasted for very good flavor; I highly recommend both.

I also used a lot of **bottled pepper sauces** for the recipes in this book. Tabasco® sells a wide range of flavors, from the well-known classic Tabasco to jalapeño, chipotle, and habanero sauces. These sauces are perfect to keep on hand, both for use in the recipes here and any time a dish needs a little "kick." I like Maille® **Dijon mustard**—it has an intense spicy flavor that so many mustards lack. I also enjoy using O® **flavored oils**. They add a hint of citrus that doesn't overpower the flavor of the food.

PESTO

Traditional **pesto** is made from fresh basil, pine nuts, garlic, Parmesan cheese, and olive oil. In recent years the definition of pesto has expanded to include other uncooked sauces made from herbs or vegetables—roasted red pepper, mint, and sun-dried tomato, just to name a few. You can find both shelf-stable and refrigerated pestos; I prefer refrigerated

brands for their freshness and prefer Cibo® Naturals and Sauces 'N'Love® for their good quality and consistency. Like dairy products, jarred pestos have expiration dates, so be sure to check the date on the jar before use.

CHEESE

For the recipes in this book, I have used packaged shredded, crumbled and sliced cheeses, so your fingers will be spared nicks and scrapes (and you won't have to clean a cheese grater). Kraft® sells a huge selection of shredded cheeses. The sizes of the packages vary, but keep in mind that 4 ounces by weight of shredded cheese equals 1 cup by volume. So, a 6-ounce package of cheese equals $1\frac{1}{2}$ cups and an 8-ounce package equals 2 cups. I have given both cup and weight measurements in the recipes, so all you have to do is open the package and pour.

Cheese crumbles are another virtually work-free way to use cheese. I have used both feta and blue cheese crumbles in the recipes. They are also ideal for use in salads and quick cheese omelets.

To clear up any confusion about Parmesan cheese, please note I have used both shredded and grated Parmesan cheese. They are not the same and therefore, not interchangeable. **Shredded parmesan** is exactly that—actual strands or small pieces of cheese. When I use shredded parmesan, I tend to use Stella®

freshly shredded Parmesan cheese. **Grated parmesan** is drier than shredded and has a fine, almost powdery, texture.

I always keep **packaged herbed cheese spreads** on hand in case I need to create an instant bread-and-cheese plate. They're usually located either in the gourmet section or the cheese case of the supermarket. Boursin® and Alouette® are the brands I used for the recipes in this book. You can find **cream cheese** in a variety of flavors, too, such as garden vegetable and chive and onion. The are easy to use and, in many cases, soft enough to work with straight out of the fridge. Try a new flavor on your bagel one morning—you won't be sorry!

PASTRY AND PHYLLO DOUGH

I always have **prebaked mini phyllo** (also spelled fillo) **dough shells** by Athens Foods in my freezer. Dufour® sells slightly larger **mini tart shells,** which hold a generous tablespoon of filling and can be baked in minutes. Sheets of **phyllo dough** are easy to work with if you show them respect—just keep the dough covered with plastic wrap and a damp towel when working with them. The key to working with **puff pastry** is to make sure it defrosts in the refrigerator before using, or the sheets will crack. If the sheets do crack at the fold, gently press the edges together and roll with a rolling pin. Pepperidge Farm® is the brand I used for all puff-pastry sheets.

SPICES, HERBS, AND DRIED CHILES

Many spice companies have increased their inventory of herbs, spices and blends, making it much easier to find more exotic dried spices and herbs. For example, McCormick® now sells both wasabi powder and Chinese five-spice powder. If you do not see the herb or spice you want, ask your supermarket to order it, or you can order it directly from the company at 800-632-5847 or online.

Dried herbs and spices should always be stored away from heat and light to maintain optimum freshness. If stored properly, most ground spices and herbs will keep their potency for 2 to 3 years. An easy way to check if a spice has lost its flavor is to smell it. If you can't smell the spice, chances are you won't be able to taste it either, so it's probably time for a new bottle.

Dried chiles have also recently become more commonly found in the supermarket spice aisle. **Ancho chiles,** which are dried poblano chiles, and **chipotle peppers,** which are dried and smoked jalapenos, are now available both whole and ground. I used the ground versions for the recipes in this book.

Many fresh herbs are available in the produce section, often in plastic clam-shell containers, but if you buy bunches of fresh herbs in season, they are less expensive.

Treat fresh herbs like you would fresh flowers: place them stem-down in water-filled jars, cover loosely with a plastic bag, and store in the refrigerator.

FRESH FRUITS AND VEGETABLES

The produce section of the supermarket offers a variety of cut-up vegetables and fruit you can use for some of these recipes or a crudité platter. Vegetables—from baby carrots to broccoli florets—only require opening the packages and arranging on a tray.

Mushrooms of all varieties are sold sliced, wrapped, and recipe-ready.

Containers of bite-sized chunks of fruits such as pineapple and different varieties of melon can usually be found in the produce section, so you don't have to peel or seed them—just open them and you're good to go.

Keep fresh fruits and vegetables in their original wrappings, which are designed to be breathable, to maintain optimum freshness until you need them.

GARLIC

Jars of peeled whole garlic can be found in the produce section. Select brands that need refrigeration and contain no additives or preservatives. Christopher Ranch® is one that has worked well for me and is easy to find. I suggest buying the smallest jar so you can maintain optimum freshness.

Many supermarkets also sell packages of peeled garlic that have been peeled on site, and might be a little fresher than the jarred brands. Either option is a time-saver and will provide fresh garlic flavor.

NUTS

Whole and chopped walnuts, almonds, pecans, and hazelnuts can be scooped straight from the package. I store them in the freezer for maximum shelf life; you don't need to defrost them before using. Just remember to taste nuts before adding them to any recipe to make sure that they are not rancid.

SEAFOOD

A bag of frozen cooked shrimp is one of the most important staples in my freezer. Be sure the shrimp are individually frozen, instead of frozen in a block—it makes it easier to measure out a particular amount.

Shrimp is sold by size—jumbo, large, medium, etc., and larger shrimp tends to be more expensive. Which size you buy depends on how you're using it. If you are cutting up shrimp for quesadillas, for example, the most economical choice is medium cooked, shelled, and deveined shrimp. Medium shrimp range in size from 40 to 70 pieces per pound.

When you're looking for smoked salmon, you'll probably find three different varieties: gravlax, nova, and lox. **Gravlax** is a salt-and-sugar-cured salmon that is both salty and slightly sweet. **Nova,** which is soaked in brine and then smoked, is the most widely available type. These days, what is sold as **lox,** the saltiest variety, is often actually nova. Be sure to taste any smoked salmon before using it, and adjust the amount of salt in the recipe if necessary.

I recommend buying smoked salmon that is pre-sliced. Ducktrap™ has excellent flavor and quality and is available in 4- to 16-ounce packages. I prefer the texture of smoked salmon that has not been frozen, which should be noted on the label.

Buy smoked trout that is filleted, but not sliced; breaking it into pieces is very easy. Look carefully at the fillet before buying it. You want fish that looks moist, not dry around the edges.

THE DELI COUNTER

I find supermarket deli sections very valuable for party planning. In addition to the cold cuts you expect, supermarket delis also offer roasted meats like chicken and ribs and a wide selection of prepared salads.

The ham and turkey sold at the deli counter are usually of higher quality than the packaged versions you'll find in the meat case. If you're unsure about which brand to choose, go for the brand with the least processing and ask for a taste. I like the quality and the flavor of Black Forest ham.

Prosciutto, Italian salt-cured ham, is now available both domestically and imported—use whichever you prefer. The Cittero® brand worked well for me and was very thinly sliced, which made it easier to wrap around figs or pears or whatever.

Pâté is a mixture of finely chopped meat and livers, usually made from pork or duck. It is available in two textures: **mousse** is the smoother texture and has a flavor that is more like liver, and **country style** (also called coarse), which has a meatier taste and texture. Both are available in various flavors, such as peppercorn and mushroom. There are also vegetarian and seafood pâtés available, if you prefer those. If you try one flavor or texture and don't enjoy it, don't be afraid to try a different one the next time; what you prefer will depend on your tastes. I like two brands: D'Artagnan® and Alexian™.

MEAT MARKET

Another area of the supermarket that has changed in recent years is the meat case. You can often find good quality packaged fully-cooked meats, such as beef and pork ribs and shredded cooked chicken and pork from Lloyd's®.

Bruce Aidell's® fully-cooked sausages—both regular and cocktail-sized—are available in many tempting flavor combinations, such as mango-chicken.

Shady Brook® turkey appetizer-size meatballs are perfect cocktail-party fare.

Perdue® Short Cuts® roasted chicken is sold in convenient premeasured 1-cup packets—how's that for time-saving?

Oscar Mayer® precooked bacon has the same great flavor of uncooked bacon, couldn't be easier to use, and there's no greasy pan to clean up afterwards.

THE CRACKER BARREL

There is a huge variety of **crackers** available these days. Don't just visit the cracker aisle—many of the most interesting crackers can be found in the gourmet or international section of the supermarket. I suggest keeping an assortment stocked in your pantry so you're always prepared. Carr's® Water Table Crackers, Vong's® Sesame Rice Crisps, New York Flatbreads®, Nejaumes® Lavasch Crackers, Ak-Mak® Whole Wheat Crackers, Starr Ridge® Crackers, Ka-Me® Rice Crunch Crackers, and Alexia™ Mini Toasts are some of my favorites.

EQUIPMENT

A well-stocked kitchen helps ease a cook's work and helps to assure that the end result is a successful recipe. For the recipes in this book, I assume you have basic equipment and know how to use it—baking sheets, measuring cups and spoons, jelly roll pans, a good set of knives, a food processor, and a blender.

In addition to the basic kitchen gear, a **microplane grater** for grating the zest of citrus fruits is a useful tool—just be careful to grate only the colored skin on the outside and avoid the bitter white pith underneath. A small tablespoon-capacity **ice cream scoop** is wonderful for shaping meatballs or scooping doughs. **Silicone bakeware** is a relatively new product on the market. I particularly like using a mini Madeleine pan for baking bite-sized cornbread. A **pastry brush** is really a must-have tool when working with puff pastry. It makes brushing melted butter evenly over dough so much easier.

PRESENTATION OF PARTY FOODS

Instead of just laying out the usual bowls for dips, consider using something a little more organic, like a hollowed-out bell pepper, red cabbage, squash, or round bread (keep the bread chunks and use them to make bread crumbs). Arrange vegetables for crudité on flat platters or trays lined with non-wilting greens such as curly endive, Savoy cabbage leaves, or red or green kale. Make sure to place veggies that have contrasting colors next to one another—place carrots next to green beans and green beans next to red pepper strips.

Another interesting platter-lining technique is to use dried legumes such as black beans or orange or red lentils to cover the surface of trays and arrange bite-sized foods on top. Consider the color of the background and the food to be placed on top. For example, black beans are an ideal background for Mini Sausage Pies.

For buffet party food, use large, flat dishes. Create even more visual interest by placing inverted bowls under the tablecloth (or cover them with napkins) to make "pedestals" of different heights.

Don't forget to place mini bowls around for discarded toothpicks and olive pits. Or place a half a lemon, cut-side up, on the tray to hold discarded toothpicks.

Use beverage-sized paper napkins for wrapping finger sandwiches such as a Croque Monsieur or use paper petit-four cups to hold small bites of food such as cheese crisps. You can find both of these items in the paper and party goods aisle of your supermarket or at your local party goods store.

FREEZER, FRIDGE, AND PANTRY

Following is a list of the ingredients I call for in the recipes in this book. Keep your favorites on hand (for your favorite recipes) and you'll always be ready to serve up something tasty for surprise guests. All that's missing are the occasional fresh ingredients: fruits, vegetables, herbs, fish, or meat.

IN THE FREEZER . . .

VEGETABLES
Alexia™ Foods Yukon Gold potatoes
Alexia™ Foods oven fries with sea salt and olive oil
Alexia™ Foods mashed potatoes
Chopped spinach
Spinach soufflé
Asparagus spears
Baby lima beans
Tiny green Peas

NUTS
Diamond® walnut halves
Diamond® walnut pieces
Diamond® raw whole almonds
Diamond® blanched sliced almonds
Diamond® pecan halves
Diamond® pecan pieces
Sugared walnuts
Raw cashews
Whole hazelnuts
Chopped hazelnuts

Chopped peanuts
Pine nuts
Sweetened flaked coconut

PASTRY
Pepperidge Farm® frozen puff pastry
Athens Foods® mini phyllo shells
Athens Foods® phyllo pastry dough
Dufour® Pastry Kitchen mini tart shells
Egg roll wrappers
Wonton wrappers

SEAFOOD
Cooked, shelled, and deveined shrimp
Cleaned calamari

IN THE REFRIGERATOR . . .

MEATS
Hormel® pepperoni
Citterio® sopressata
Citterio® prosciutto
Oscar Mayer® precooked bacon slices
Deli corned beef
Black Forest ham
Deli good-quality sliced ham
Deli cooked turkey
Deli sliced roast beef
Alexian™ truffle mousse
Alexian™ pâté de campagne
Perdue® Short Cuts® roasted chicken
Lloyd's® fully-cooked baby back ribs
Lloyd's® fully-cooked beef ribs
Lloyd's® fully-cooked shredded beef

Lloyd's® fully-cooked shredded chicken
Shady Brook® appetizer-size turkey
  meatballs
Hebrew National® all-beef cocktail franks
Bruce Aidell's® chicken and apple sausage
Bruce Aidell's® cocktail sausages
Chorizo sausages
Kielbasa

CHEESES
Stella® freshly shredded Parmesan cheese
Grated Parmesan cheese
Kraft® Philadelphia cream cheese
Kraft® Philadelphia salmon cream cheese
Kraft® Philadelphia herb-and-garlic
  cream cheese
Kraft® Philadelphia chive-and-onion
  cream cheese
Kraft® Philadelphia jalapeño cream cheese
Kraft® Philadelphia garden vegetable cream
  cheese
Kraft® shredded Cheddar cheese
Kraft® shredded Mexican 4-cheese blend
  (Cheddar, Monterey Jack, queso blanco,
  and asadero)
Kraft® shredded Cheddar and Jack blend
Kraft® shredded Swiss cheese
Kraft® shredded Mozzarella cheese
Goat cheese
Alouette® herb cheese
Boursin® herb-garlic cheese
Boursin® pepper-herb cheese
Feta cheese crumbles
Basil-and-tomato feta cheese crumbles
Garlic-and-herb feta cheese crumbles

Blue cheese crumbles
Provolone
Mascarpone
Ricotta
Brie, a 2.2-pound wheel
Dill havarti
Caraway havarti
Gorgonzola
Roquefort
Asiago
Gruyère
Bocconcini (mini mozzarella)
Mozzarella cheese sticks

BREADS AND DOUGHS
Tyson® flour tortillas
Tyson® corn tortillas
Pillsbury® refrigerated crescent rolls
Melissa's® crepes
Mini blini

DAIRY
Sour cream
Crème fraîche
Butter
Eggs
Milk
Heavy cream
Plain yogurt
Buttermilk

SEAFOOD
Ducktrap™ smoked salmon
Ducktrap™ smoked trout fillet
Ducktrap™ salmon gravlax
Vita® herring in wine sauce

SAUCES
Cibo Naturals® classic pesto
Cibo Naturals® roasted red pepper pesto
Cibo Naturals® sundried tomato pesto
Sauce 'N' Love™ basil pesto
Sauce 'N' Love™ mint pesto

MISCELLANEOUS
Fresh peeled whole garlic
   (Christopher Ranch® or Melissa's®)
Minced garlic
Chopped garlic
Shredded potatoes
Sauerkraut
Orange juice

IN THE PANTRY . . .

SAUCES, CONDIMENTS, AND MARINADES
(refrigerate after opening)
Green Mountain® salsa
Frontera® chipotle salsa
Frontera® roasted tomato salsa
Frontera® tomatillo salsa
Kikkoman® soy sauce
Tabasco® sauce
Tabasco® jalapeño sauce

Tabasco® chipotle sauce
Maille® Dijon mustard
Honey mustard
K.C. Masterpiece® ginger and garlic marinade
Prepared horseradish
Mayonnaise
Ketchup
Teriyaki sauce
Pizza sauce
Duck sauce
Barbecue sauce
Tartar sauce
Marinara sauce
Blue cheese dressing
Russian dressing
Balsamic vinaigrette

CANNED GOODS
Swanson® chicken broth
Del Monte® chopped tomatoes
Del Monte® diced tomatoes with
   garlic and olive oil
Sliced water chestnuts
Chopped green chiles
Sliced pickled jalapeño peppers
Black-eyed peas
Black beans
Chickpeas
Whole kernel corn
Libby's® Mexicorn
Artichoke hearts in water
White tuna in water
Pineapple chunks
Coconut milk (unsweetened)

Whole-berry cranberry sauce
Anchovy fillets
Pitted whole black olives
Sliced black olives

BREADS AND BAKING GOODS
Pillsbury® Pie Crust mix
General Mills® all-purpose baking mix
Quaker® masa harina
McCormick® all-purpose batter fry mix
Pillsbury® hot roll mix
Jiffy® corn bread mix
Matzo meal
Rice paper
Boboli® small pizza crusts
Pepperidge Farm® party rye
Pepperidge Farm® white sandwich bread
Pumpernickel bread
White party rolls
Pita bread
Semolina bread
Tortilla chips
Carr's® Water Table Crackers
Vong's® Sesame Rice Crisps
New York Flatbreads®
Nejaimes® Lavasch Crackers
Ak-Mak® Whole Wheat Crackers
Starr Ridge® Crackers
Ka-Me® Rice Crunch Crackers
Alexia™ Mini Toasts

JAMS, JELLIES, AND SPREADS
(refrigerate after opening)
Sesame tahini
Capers
Black olive spread
Stonewall Kitchens® lemon curd
Lulu® fig-cherry preserves
Grape jelly
Orange marmalade
Stonewall Kitchens® roasted garlic-onion jam
Red pepper jelly
Creamy peanut butter
Nutella® chocolate hazelnut spread
Honey
Lulu® white truffle honey
Anchovy paste

OILS AND VINEGARS
O® lemon-flavored oil
O® orange-flavored oil
Olive oil
Vegetable oil
Balsamic vinegar
White balsamic vinegar
Red wine vinegar

SPICE SHELF AND DRY GOODS
Morton's™ hot salt
McCormick® wasabi powder
McCormick® five-spice seasoning,
McCormick® chipotle chile pepper
McCormick® ancho chile pepper
K.C. Masterpiece® BBQ seasoning
Taco seasoning mix

Lipton® onion soup mix
Ranch salad dressing and dip mix
Patak's® curry paste
Crushed red pepper
Chili powder
Curry powder
Fennel seeds
Black pepper
White pepper
Bay leaves
Star anise
Dried basil
Dried oregano
Dried thyme
Dried tarragon
Dried rosemary
Dried dill weed
Dry mustard
Ground cayenne
Ground nutmeg
Ground cumin
Ground paprika
Ground ginger
Garlic salt
Kosher salt
Ground cinnamon
Cinnamon sugar
Granulated sugar
Light brown sugar
Confectioners' sugar
All-purpose flour
Semisweet chocolate
Vanilla extract

Knox® original unflavored gelatin
Pitted dates
Dried cranberries

MISCELLANEOUS
(refrigerate after opening)
Red caviar
Lumpfish caviar
Salmon caviar
Pickled sliced ginger
Kalamata olives
Pimiento-stuffed olives
Pitted Niçoise olives
L'Esprit Compagne® sun-dried tomatoes in oil
Roasted red pepper

WINE/LIQUOR
Red wine
Anise-flavored liqueur
Calvados
Vodka
Gin
Scotch whisky
Tequila
White wine
Beer
Sherry

Dive In

Red-Alert Dip

Roasting really brings out the sweet flavor of the beets.

PREP TIME: 15 MINUTES • BAKE TIME: 30 MINUTES • MAKES: 1¼ CUPS

4 medium canned whole beets
¼ teaspoon grated lemon zest
2 tablespoons lemon juice
¾ cup mayonnaise
1 teaspoon sugar
¼ teaspoon salt
Assorted fresh vegetables, for serving

1. Heat oven to 400°F. Place beets in an ovenproof dish and roast 30 minutes; let cool.

2. Place cooled beets, lemon zest and juice, mayonnaise, and seasonings in a blender container; cover and purée until smooth, stopping the blender occasionally to scrape down sides of the container. (Can be made ahead, covered, and refrigerated up to 2 days.) Serve with assorted fresh vegetables.

Creamy Blue Cheese Dip

Use your favorite blue cheese—Roquefort, Gorgonzola, Danish, Stilton—for this easy dip.

PREP TIME: 10 MINUTES • MAKES: 1½ CUPS

1 container (8 ounces) chive-and-onion cream cheese
4 ounces blue cheese
⅓ cup sour cream
2 tablespoons butter
Assorted crackers, for serving

In the bowl of a food processor with the steel blade attached, combine cream cheese, blue cheese, sour cream, and butter. Process until smooth, stopping the machine occasionally to scrape down the sides of the bowl. Spoon mixture into a bowl, cover, and refrigerate until serving time. (Can be made ahead, covered, and refrigerated up to 2 days.) Serve with assorted crackers.

Curry Dip

This versatile dip works well not only with vegetables but also with chicken or shrimp. For the best flavor, make a day ahead.

PREP TIME: 15 MINUTES • **MAKES: 1½ CUPS**

1 cup mayonnaise
¼ cup sour cream
¼ cup plain yogurt
4 teaspoons curry powder
2 teaspoons sugar
1 teaspoon salt
½ teaspoon minced garlic
Fresh vegetables, for serving

In a medium bowl, combine all ingredients except the vegetables and stir until well combined. Cover and refrigerate up to 24 hours. (Can be made ahead, covered, and refrigerated up to 3 days.) Serve with assorted vegetables, such as blanched broccoli and cauliflower, zucchini and yellow squash slices, and bell pepper strips.

Spicy Peanut Dip

If you have any of this dip left over, toss it with cooked noodles for an Asian-inspired side dish for grilled chicken.

PREP TIME: 10 MINUTES • MAKES: 1 1/2 CUPS

1 cup creamy peanut butter
2 tablespoons soy sauce
2 tablespoons white vinegar
2 teaspoons chopped garlic
1 1/2 teaspoons chopped pickled ginger
1 teaspoon Asian sesame oil
1/8 teaspoon bottled hot sauce
1/4 cup hot water
Fresh vegetables, for serving

In the bowl of a food processor with the steel blade attached, combine all ingredients except the water and fresh vegetables. Pulse until well mixed, stopping the machine occasionally to scrape down the sides of the bowl. With the motor running, add the hot water through the feed tube and process until smooth. Serve with fresh vegetables, such as snow peas, blanched broccoli, and bell pepper strips.

Classic Onion Soup Dip

Yes! This is the two-ingredient dip that we all love and serve!

PREP TIME: 5 MINUTES • MAKES: 2 CUPS

1 envelope (1 ounce) onion soup mix
1 container (16 ounces) sour cream
Potato chips, for serving

In a medium bowl, combine soup mix and sour cream. Stir until well mixed. Cover and refrigerate until ready to serve. Serve with potato chips.

Lima Bean Dip

The delicate flavor of the bean is enhanced by pancetta and sage. Be sure to use baby limas—they are more tender than the Fordhook variety.

PREP TIME: 20 MINUTES • MAKES: 1 ½ CUPS

1 package (10 ounces) baby lima beans, thawed
¼ cup chicken broth
1 garlic clove, peeled
¼ cup cooked, diced pancetta, or 2 slices cooked bacon, crumbled
2 tablespoons olive oil
½ teaspoon salt
½ teaspoon dried sage
1 loaf crusty bread, sliced, for serving

1. In a medium saucepan, combine lima beans, chicken broth, and garlic and cook for 5 minutes.

2. Pour lima bean mixture into the bowl of a food processor with the steel blade attached; pulse until chopped.

3. Add pancetta, olive oil, and seasonings. Continue pulsing until smooth, stopping the machine occasionally to scrape down the sides of the bowl. (Can be made ahead, covered, and refrigerated up to 3 days. Bring to room temperature 30 minutes before serving.) Serve at room temperature with crusty bread slices.

Creamy Spinach Dip

The consistency of this dip varies depending on how much moisture you squeeze out of the spinach.

PREP TIME: 20 MINUTES • **MAKES: 3 CUPS**

1 package (10 ounces) frozen chopped spinach, thawed and drained
1 ½ cups mayonnaise
½ cup sour cream
½ cup packed parsley leaves
½ cup chopped green onions
½ teaspoon salt
⅛ teaspoon Worcestershire sauce
Assorted fresh vegetables, for serving

1. Place the spinach in a colander and squeeze out the moisture with the back of a large spoon.

2. In the bowl of a food processor with the steel blade attached, combine spinach and remaining ingredients except the raw vegetables. Pulse until well mixed and spinach is uniformly minced, stopping the machine occasionally to scrape down the sides of the bowl. (Can be made ahead, covered, and refrigerated up to 24 hours.) Serve with assorted fresh vegetables.

Minted Green Pea Dip

The tinier the peas, the better, because their skin is more tender.

PREP TIME: **15 MINUTES** • MAKES: **1¼ CUPS**

1 package (10 ounces) tiny tender
　　green peas, thawed
3 slices precooked bacon
¼ cup packed fresh mint leaves
3 tablespoons olive oil
¼ teaspoon salt
Fresh vegetables, for serving
Sliced bread, toasted, for serving

1. Place peas in a medium bowl, pour hot water over, and let stand 1 minute; drain. Heat bacon in microwave according to package directions; crumble.

2. In the bowl of a food processor with the steel blade attached, combine peas, bacon, mint, olive oil, and salt. Pulse until smooth, stopping the machine occasionally to scrape down the sides of the bowl. If mixture is too thick, add a drop or two of water. (Can be made ahead, covered, and refrigerated up to 2 days. Let stand at room temperature 30 minutes before serving.) Serve with assorted vegetables and a variety of toasted bread slices.

Taramasalata

This dip is traditionally made with tarama, which is pale orange carp roe. We substitute red caviar—it's much easier to find.

PREP TIME: 15 MINUTES • **MAKES: 1 ½ CUPS**

1 cup prepared mashed potatoes
⅓ cup chive-and-onion cream cheese
1 jar (2 ounces) red lumpfish caviar
¼ cup ground blanched almonds
3 tablespoons fresh lemon juice
Pita bread, split and cut into wedges, or assorted crackers, for serving

1. Place mashed potatoes in a medium microwaveproof bowl. Cover with a paper towel and heat 1 minute; stir until smooth.

2. Add cream cheese and stir until combined.

3. Fold in caviar, ground almonds, and lemon juice. Cover and refrigerate until well chilled. (Can be made ahead, covered, and refrigerated up to 24 hours.) Serve with pita bread or assorted crackers.

Skordalia

This Greek dip should be very garlicky and lemony.

PREP TIME: 10 MINUTES • **MICROWAVE TIME: 1 MINUTE** • **MAKES: 1 CUP**

1 cup prepared mashed potatoes
1 1/2 teaspoons chopped garlic
3 tablespoons olive oil
2 tablespoons fresh lemon juice
1/4 teaspoon salt
Pita chips, for serving

1. In a medium microwaveproof bowl, combine mashed potatoes and garlic. Cover bowl with a paper towel and microwave for 1 minute. Stir.

2. Add olive oil and stir gently. Stir in lemon juice and salt. Taste for seasoning and add more salt, if needed. Serve warm or at room temperature with pita chips.

Romesco Sauce

This robust Mediterranean sauce traditionally includes fire-roasted tomatoes. It's also a delicious alternative to cocktail sauce for boiled shrimp.

PREP TIME: 20 MINUTES • MAKES: 2½ CUPS

¼ cup blanched almonds, toasted and finely ground

¼ cup toasted hazelnuts, skinned and finely ground

2 slices fresh bread, cubed (about ⅔ cup)

1½ cups prepared mild roasted tomato salsa

1 tablespoon olive oil

Toasted bread slices, for serving

1. Place nuts and bread cubes in the bowl of a food processor with the steel blade attached. Pulse until nuts and bread are equally fine.

2. Add the salsa and olive oil; pulse again, stopping the machine occasionally to scrape down the sides of the bowl. (Can be made ahead, covered, and refrigerated up to 3 days. Stir before serving.) Serve with toasted bread.

Smoked Salmon Dip

A brine-cured, cold-smoked salmon was used for this recipe. It can be found in the deli section of many supermarkets.

PREP TIME: 20 MINUTES • MAKES: 1 ½ CUPS

1 container (8 ounces) chive-and-
onion cream cheese, softened
4 ounces sliced smoked salmon,
chopped
1 tablespoon fresh lemon juice
1 tablespoon chopped fresh dill
1 tablespoon drained capers
Mini bagels or cucumber slices,
for serving

In the bowl of a food processor with the steel blade attached, combine the cream cheese, smoked salmon, lemon juice, dill, and capers. Pulse until mixed, stopping the machine occasionally to scrape down the sides of the bowl. Spoon into a small bowl, cover, and refrigerate at least 2 hours for flavors to blend. (Can be made ahead, covered, and refrigerated up to 24 hours.) Serve with mini bagels or cucumber slices.

Hummus

Tahini gives this thick Middle Eastern dip its nutty flavor.

PREP TIME: 10 MINUTES • **MAKES: 1 ½ CUPS**

1 can (15.5 ounces) chickpeas,
    drained
¼ cup tahini (sesame seed paste); stir
    well before measuring
2 tablespoons fresh lemon juice
2 tablespoons olive oil
1 teaspoon chopped garlic
½ teaspoon salt
1 to 2 tablespoons water, or as
    needed
Pita bread, split and cut into wedges,
    for serving

1. In the bowl of a food processor with the steel blade attached, combine all the ingredients except the pita bread.

2. Pulse until smooth, stopping the machine occasionally to scrape down the sides of the bowl. If dip is too thick, add water until it is the consistency of thick sour cream. Serve with pita bread wedges.

Tzatziki

This Greek sauce made from yogurt and cucumbers is great both as a dip and as a condiment for fried foods.

PREP TIME: 30 MINUTES • MAKES: 3½ CUPS

1 English or European cucumber,
    peeled and seeded
2 cups plain yogurt
4 teaspoons minced garlic
1 tablespoon olive oil
1 tablespoon white vinegar
1 teaspoon salt
½ cup chopped fresh mint or dill
Pita bread, split and cut into wedges,
    or fresh vegetables, for serving

1. Using a cheese grater, shred the cucumber into a colander. Drain for 15 minutes, pressing out moisture with the back of a spoon.

2. Line a strainer with a coffee filter, pour in the yogurt, and drain over a bowl for 30 minutes.

3. In a large bowl, combine cucumber, yogurt, garlic, olive oil, vinegar, salt, and mint. Stir until well combined. Cover and refrigerate for at least 2 hours before serving. Serve with pita wedges or fresh vegetables.

Baba Ghanoush

Even people who don't love eggplant will enjoy this Mediterranean dip.

PREP TIME: 10 MINUTES • BAKE TIME: 40 MINUTES • MAKES: 1 CUP

2 eggplants, about 1½ pounds total
2 tablespoons tahini (sesame seed
     paste); stir before measuring
1 tablespoon fresh lemon juice
1 tablespoon olive oil
1 garlic clove, chopped
1 teaspoon salt
Pita bread, split and cut into wedges,
     for serving

1. Heat oven to 400°F. Cut each eggplant in half lengthwise. Place, cut-side down, on a lightly oiled baking sheet. Bake for 40 minutes or until eggplant is tender. Cool to room temperature.

2. With a spoon, remove and discard the seeds (they make the dip bitter). Scrape the remaining eggplant pulp into the bowl of a food processor with the steel blade attached. Add tahini, lemon juice, olive oil, garlic, and salt, and pulse until mixture is smooth. (Can be made ahead, covered, and refrigerated up to 24 hours.) Serve with pita bread wedges.

Tapenade

This Provençal olive paste is addictive. Orange peel brightens up the flavor of the prepared olive spread.

PREP TIME: 5 MINUTES • MAKES: 1 CUP

1 jar (8 ounces) prepared black olive spread
1 tablespoon chopped parsley
1 teaspoon grated orange zest
½ teaspoon chopped garlic
Assorted crackers, for serving

In a small bowl, combine all ingredients except crackers; stir until well mixed. Let stand for 1 hour for flavors to blend. Serve with assorted crackers.

Baked Reuben Dip

All the wonderful flavors of a grilled Reuben sandwich baked to gooey perfection.

PREP TIME: 15 MINUTES • **BAKE TIME: 35 MINUTES** • **MAKES: 32 SERVINGS**

1 package (8 ounces) refrigerated
   sauerkraut
½ pound sliced lean corned beef,
   chopped
1 package (8 ounces) shredded Swiss
   cheese
1 package (8 ounces) shredded
   Cheddar cheese
1 cup mayonnaise
1 package (16 ounces) sliced cocktail
   rye bread

1. Heat oven to 350°F. Drain sauerkraut in a colander, rinse with cold water, and drain again. In a large bowl, combine the drained sauerkraut, corned beef, both cheeses, and mayonnaise; stir.

2. Spoon mixture into a 13 x 9-inch shallow baking dish. Bake for 30 minutes.

3. Just before serving, arrange the rye bread on a baking sheet and toast. Serve dip hot with toasted bread.

Spicy Artichoke Dip

After Classic Onion Soup Dip, this is probably the second most-loved party dip. Use the artichokes packed in water.

PREP TIME: 20 MINUTES • BAKE TIME: 30 MINUTES • MAKES: 3 1/2 CUPS

1 can (14 ounces) artichoke hearts, drained
1 cup (4 ounces) shredded Parmesan cheese
1 cup mayonnaise
1 package (8 ounces) cream cheese, softened
1/4 teaspoon bottled red pepper sauce
1 tablespoon chopped parsley, for garnish
Assorted crackers, for serving

1. In the bowl of a food processor with the steel blade attached, combine all ingredients except the parsley and crackers. Pulse until finely chopped, stopping the machine occasionally to scrape down the sides of the bowl.

2. Heat oven to 350°F. Spoon mixture into a shallow 4-cup flan or quiche dish, or 9-inch pie plate. Bake 30 minutes until lightly browned and bubbly. Garnish with parsley and serve with assorted crackers.

VARIATIONS

Spicy Spinach Dip
Omit the artichokes and substitute 1 package (10 ounces) frozen chopped spinach, thawed and well drained, and add 1/4 teaspoon ground nutmeg. Bake as directed above.

Spicy Crab-Artichoke Dip
Add 8 ounces real or imitation crabmeat (surimi). Bake as directed above.

Roquefort-Walnut Dip

Pears are a perfect accompaniment to this dip.

PREP TIME: 5 MINUTES • **BAKE TIME: 10 MINUTES** • **MAKES: 1½ CUPS**

½ cup chopped walnuts
4 ounces Roquefort cheese
1 cup sour cream
2 Bosc pears, cut into 8 wedges each,
    for serving

1. Heat oven to 350°F. Place nuts on a baking pan in a single layer and toast for 10 minutes. Let cool to room temperature.

2. Crumble the cheese into a medium bowl. Add the sour cream and stir until combined. Fold in the nuts. Spoon mixture into a serving bowl. (Can be made ahead, covered, and refrigerated up to 2 days. Let stand at room temperature for 30 minutes before serving.) Serve at room temperature with pear wedges.

Black-Eyed Pea Dip

This dip is sometimes called Texas or Carolina caviar. Whatever it is called, it will be called delicious as well.

PREP TIME: 15 MINUTES • MAKES: 5 CUPS

2 cans (15.5 ounces) black-eyed peas, drained and rinsed
1 medium onion, chopped
1 medium red bell pepper, diced
1 jalapeño pepper, minced
1 teaspoon minced garlic
1 bottle (8 ounces) balsamic vinaigrette
Tortilla chips, for serving

In a large bowl, combine all ingredients except tortilla chips. Toss until well mixed. Refrigerate at least 5 hours before serving for flavors to blend. (Can be made ahead, covered, and refrigerated up to 2 days.) Serve with tortilla chips.

Zesty Pecan Dip with Roasted New Potatoes

Plan ahead for this dip—it's so much better when flavors are allowed to mellow for a day.

PREP TIME: 20 MINUTES • BAKE TIME: 45 MINUTES • MAKES: 2½ CUPS

2 cups sour cream
½ cup finely chopped toasted pecans
½ cup finely chopped parsley
1 teaspoon minced garlic
½ teaspoon paprika
1 tablespoon olive oil
2 pounds small new potatoes, halved
½ teaspoon hot salt
1 teaspoon kosher salt

1. In a medium bowl, combine the sour cream, pecans, parsley, garlic, and paprika; stir to mix. Cover and refrigerate for 24 hours to allow flavors to blend. (Can be made ahead, covered, and refrigerated up to 3 days.)

2. Heat oven to 425°F. Coat a roasting pan with oil and heat for 3 minutes. Add potatoes, hot salt, and kosher salt and roast until fork-tender, about 20 minutes. Transfer potatoes to a serving bowl. Spoon dip into another bowl and serve.

Bacon and Tomato Dip

The perfect marriage of flavors: bacon and tomatoes. In the off-season, use cherry tomatoes—they still pack intense tomato flavor even in the depths of winter.

PREP TIME: 20 MINUTES • **MAKES: 12 SERVINGS**

6 slices precooked bacon (about ½ cup crumbled)

1 medium tomato, chopped (about ½ pound)

1 package (8 ounces) cream cheese, softened

¼ cup mayonnaise

2 tablespoons chopped fresh basil

⅛ teaspoon freshly ground pepper

1 baguette, sliced and toasted, for serving

1. Heat bacon in microwave according to package directions; crumble.

2. In the bowl of a food processor with the steel blade attached, combine bacon, tomato, cream cheese, mayonnaise, basil, and pepper. Pulse until smooth, stopping the machine occasionally to scrape down the sides of the bowl. Serve with toasted bread slices. For an elegant presentation, spoon rounded tablespoons onto the ends of endive leaves and arrange in a circle on a serving tray.

Cumin-White Bean Dip

The combination of canned beans and the food processor makes quick work of this white bean dip.

PREP TIME: 20 MINUTES • MAKES: 1½ CUPS

1 can (15.5 ounces) white beans,
     rinsed and drained
¼ cup olive oil
3 tablespoons chopped cilantro
2 tablespoons fresh lemon juice
2 teaspoons minced garlic
1½ teaspoons ground cumin
1 teaspoon hot pepper sauce
¼ teaspoon salt
Cilantro, for garnish
Tortilla chips or assorted fresh
     vegetables, for serving

In the bowl of a food processor with the steel blade attached, combine the beans, olive oil, chopped cilantro, lemon juice, garlic, cumin, hot sauce, and salt. Pulse until smooth, stopping the machine occasionally to scrape down the sides of the bowl. Cover and refrigerate up to 24 hours to let flavors develop. Garnish with cilantro and serve with tortilla chips or fresh vegetables.

Black Bean Dip

For bean dip at the atomic heat level, just use the spiciest salsa you can find.

PREP TIME: 15 MINUTES • **MAKES: 1 ½ CUPS**

1 can (15½ ounces) black beans
½ cup prepared salsa
1 tablespoon fresh lime juice
1 teaspoon bottled chipotle sauce
Tortilla chips, for serving

1. Rinse beans under cold water to remove starchy bean liquid. Drain well.

2. In the bowl of a food processor with the steel blade attached, combine beans, salsa, lime juice, and hot sauce. Pulse until smooth, stopping occasionally to scrape down the sides of the bowl. Spoon into a serving bowl. (Can be made ahead, covered, and refrigerated up to 2 days. Bring to room temperature before serving.) Serve with tortilla chips.

Chorizo-Cheese Dip

If you serve this dip on a buffet table, be sure to keep it warm.

PREP TIME: 5 MINUTES • **COOK TIME: 2 MINUTES** • **MAKES: 2½ CUPS**

1 dried, ready-to-eat chorizo sausage,
    finely chopped (⅓ cup)
⅓ cup chopped green onions
½ cup chicken broth
1 package (16 ounces) shredded
    Mexican-style four-cheese mix
    (Cheddar, Monterey Jack, queso
    blanco, and asadero)
Tortilla chips, for serving

1. In a microwaveproof bowl, combine sausage, green onions, and broth; cover and microwave for 1 minute.

2. Add cheese; cover and microwave for 1 minute more; stir. If the cheese has not melted completely, microwave at 15-second intervals until completely melted. Serve with tortilla chips. Reheat if necessary in the microwave, heating only in 30-second intervals.

DIVE IN

Strawberry-Tomato Salsa

This fun, unusual salsa also pairs very well with grilled chicken or fish.

PREP TIME: **30 MINUTES** • MAKES: **4 CUPS**

3 tablespoons olive oil

1 ½ tablespoons white balsamic vinegar

¾ teaspoon salt

1 pint cherry tomatoes, chopped

1 cup chopped strawberries

4 green onions, finely chopped

¼ cup chopped fresh cilantro

Tortilla chips, for serving

1. In a large bowl, combine olive oil, vinegar, and salt; whisk until well blended.

2. Add tomatoes, strawberries, green onions, and cilantro; toss until well mixed. Cover and refrigerate for 1 hour. (Can be made ahead, covered, and refrigerated up to 24 hours.) Serve with tortilla chips.

VARIATION

Cherry-Tomato Salsa
Substitute 1 cup pitted, chopped sweet cherries for the strawberries. Add 2 teaspoons minced fresh jalapeño pepper.

Guacamole

To ensure a ripe avocado, purchase 3 or 4 days ahead and ripen at room temperature.

PREP TIME: **10 MINUTES** • MAKES: **1 ¼ CUPS**

1 ripe avocado, peeled and pit
   removed
½ cup prepared salsa
2 tablespoons chopped cilantro
1 tablespoon fresh lime juice
½ teaspoon salt
¼ teaspoon bottled red pepper sauce
Tortilla chips, for serving

Mash the avocado with a fork in a medium bowl. Stir in remaining ingredients except tortilla chips. Serve immediately. (If not serving immediately, cover the surface of the dip directly with plastic wrap to avoid discoloration.)

Salsa Verde

Tomatillos resemble green tomatoes, but are actually related to the gooseberry.

PREP TIME: 10 MINUTES • MAKES: 2½ CUPS

1 jar (16 ounces) roasted tomatillo
　salsa
½ cup chopped fresh cilantro
1 teaspoon sugar
Tortilla chips, for serving

In a medium bowl, combine salsa, cilantro, and sugar; stir to mix. (Can be made ahead. Cover and refrigerate up to 2 days.) Serve with tortilla chips.

Shrimp and Jícama Salsa

Jícama, a brown-skinned root vegetable, has a shape much like a turnip. Peel off the tough outer brown skin, then chop.

PREP TIME: 25 MINUTES • MAKES: 4 CUPS

½ pound frozen cooked, shelled,
    and deveined shrimp, thawed
    and chopped
1½ cups prepared salsa
1 cup finely chopped jícama
2 tablespoons fresh lime juice
2 tablespoons chopped fresh mint
    or cilantro
Tortilla chips, for serving

In medium bowl, combine shrimp, salsa, jícama, lime juice, and chopped mint. Cover and chill for 2 hours before serving. Serve with tortilla chips.

Warm Chile Con Queso

There is such a wide array of packaged shredded cheeses on the market no one needs to shred a cheese again! Make sure this dip stays warm if serving it on a buffet table.

PREP TIME: **20 MINUTES** • COOK TIME: **8 MINUTES** • MAKES: **2 CUPS**

1 tablespoon olive oil

½ cup drained canned diced tomatoes or 1 medium tomato, seeded and chopped (about ½ pound)

½ cup finely chopped onion

1 fresh medium jalapeño pepper, chopped

½ cup chicken broth

1 package (16 ounces) shredded Mexican-style cheese (Cheddar and Monterey Jack)

Tortilla chips, for serving

1. In a medium saucepan, heat olive oil. Add tomato, onion, and jalapeño; cook 2 minutes. Add broth and continue cooking for 5 more minutes.

2. Remove saucepan from heat and add the cheese all at once. Stir until cheese is melted. Serve with tortilla chips. Reheat if necessary in the microwave, heating only in 30-second intervals.

Mexicorn Dip

Canned Mexicorn is the base for this addictive dip. Serve with tortilla chips.

PREP TIME: 15 MINUTES • MAKES: 2 ½ CUPS

1 can (11 ounces) Mexicorn, drained
1 cup mayonnaise
1 ½ cups (6 ounces) shredded
    Mexican-style cheese (Cheddar
    and Monterey Jack)
¼ cup chopped green onions
2 tablespoons finely chopped fresh
    jalapeño pepper
1 teaspoon bottled jalapeño sauce
Tortilla chips, for serving

1. In a medium bowl, combine Mexicorn and mayonnaise; stir to combine. Fold in remaining ingredients except tortilla chips; stir until well mixed.

2. Cover bowl and refrigerate until chilled. (Can be made ahead, covered, and refrigerated up to 2 days.) Serve with tortilla chips.

Crab Bake

Use either real or imitation crabmeat—regardless, this recipe is a definite crowd pleaser.

PREP TIME: 15 MINUTES • **BAKE TIME: 30 MINUTES** • **MAKES: 3½ CUPS**

1 cup mayonnaise
1 package (8 ounces) cream cheese, softened
½ cup chopped onion
1 tablespoon fresh lemon juice
¼ teaspoon bottled hot pepper sauce
1 pound crabmeat (real or imitation)
1 tablespoon chopped parsley, for garnish
Assorted crackers, for serving

1. Heat oven to 350°F. In a medium bowl, combine all ingredients except the crabmeat, parsley, and crackers. Stir until smooth. Fold in crabmeat.

2. Spoon mixture into a shallow 4-cup quiche or 9-inch glass pie plate. Bake until lightly browned and bubbly, about 30 minutes. Garnish with parsley. Serve with assorted crackers.

VARIATION

Crab-Horseradish Bake
Add 1 tablespoon prepared horseradish to ingredients and bake as directed above.

Two-Onion Soufflé

Assemble this dip the day before and bake 30 minutes before the party begins. You might want to make extra; otherwise, you won't have any leftovers.

PREP TIME: 10 MINUTES • BAKE TIME: 30 MINUTES • MAKES: 8 TO 10 SERVINGS

1 package (8 ounces) cream cheese, softened
1 cup finely chopped onions
¼ cup mayonnaise
1 cup (4 ounces) shredded Parmesan cheese
2 tablespoons chopped green onions, for garnish
Assorted crackers, for serving

1. In a medium bowl, combine cream cheese, onions, and mayonnaise and stir until well combined. Add Parmesan and stir until well mixed. Spoon mixture into a 4-cup shallow quiche dish. (Can be made ahead, covered, and refrigerated up to 24 hours.)

2. Heat oven to 350°F. Bake for 25 to 30 minutes until lightly browned and bubbly. Garnish with green onions. Serve with assorted crackers.

Tomato Jam

This tomatoey spread is a perfect topping for garlic bread.

PREP TIME: 5 MINUTES • **COOK TIME: 20 MINUTES** • **MAKES: 1 CUP**

1 tablespoon olive oil

¼ cup sliced shallots

1 can (14.5 ounces) diced tomatoes

2 tablespoons minced sun-dried
    tomatoes packed in oil

1 tablespoon chopped pickled ginger

½ teaspoon salt

½ teaspoon sugar

2 tablespoons chopped fresh basil

Garlic bread slices, for serving

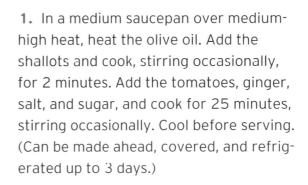

1. In a medium saucepan over medium-high heat, heat the olive oil. Add the shallots and cook, stirring occasionally, for 2 minutes. Add the tomatoes, ginger, salt, and sugar, and cook for 25 minutes, stirring occasionally. Cool before serving. (Can be made ahead, covered, and refrigerated up to 3 days.)

2. Just before serving, stir in fresh basil. Serve at room temperature with garlic bread slices.

Two-Pesto Torta

The layers of cream cheese, basil pesto, and red pepper pesto look lovely and will definitely impress your guests.

PREP TIME: 20 MINUTES • **MAKES: 10 TO 12 SERVINGS**

1 package (8 ounces) cream cheese, softened
1 cup mascarpone cheese, softened
4 tablespoons unsalted butter, softened
6 tablespoons prepared basil pesto
6 tablespoons prepared roasted red pepper pesto
Basil sprigs, for garnish (optional)
Assorted crackers, for serving

1. In a small bowl, combine the cream cheese, mascarpone, and butter; stir until smooth.

2. Line a 4-cup bowl or small loaf pan with plastic wrap. Spread one-third of the cheese mixture on the bottom. Top with basil pesto. Spread one-third of the cheese mixture over the pesto. Top with the red pepper pesto. Spread with remaining cheese mixture. Cover and refrigerate for at least 5 hours. (Can be made ahead, covered, and refrigerated up to 2 days.)

3. To serve, invert bowl onto serving plate; peel off the plastic wrap and discard. Garnish with fresh basil sprigs, if desired. Serve with assorted crackers.

Sun-Dried Tomato-Goat Cheese Spread

Using the sun-dried tomatoes packed in oil means you won't need to rehydrate them.

PREP TIME: 10 MINUTES • MAKES: 1 CUP

2 tablespoons minced sun-dried
 tomatoes packed in oil
8 ounces fresh goat cheese
2 tablespoons chopped fresh basil
½ teaspoon salt
¼ teaspoon freshly ground pepper
Assorted crackers or sliced, toasted
 bread, for serving

In the bowl of a food processor with the steel blade attached, combine all the ingredients except crackers. Pulse until smooth, stopping the machine occasionally to scrape down the sides of the bowl. Spoon mixture into a serving bowl. Serve with crackers or toasted bread slices.

Fruit Salsa with Cinnamon Crisps

This could be a whimsical dessert after a Mexican meal.

PREP TIME: 15 MINUTES • MAKES: 2 ½ CUPS

2 medium Granny Smith apples,
    peeled and cored
¼ cup orange juice
1 kiwifruit, peeled and chopped
1 cup sliced strawberries
2 tablespoons orange marmalade
4 flour tortillas
1 tablespoon cinnamon sugar

1. In the bowl of a food processor with the steel blade attached, combine the apples and orange juice; pulse until the apples are chopped. Add the kiwifruit, strawberries, and marmalade, and pulse until combined. Transfer to a bowl.

2. Meanwhile, heat the oven to 375°F. Cut each tortilla into 8 wedges and arrange on a baking sheet. Lightly sprinkle the tortillas with water, then sprinkle with cinnamon sugar. Bake for 5 minutes or until light brown and crisp. Let cool before serving.

Citrus Cream with Fruit Kabobs

A bit of sweet flavor can be a welcome taste treat on a savory buffet table.

PREP TIME: 10 MINUTES • MAKES: 1 CUP SAUCE

1 cup sour cream

2 tablespoons sugar

2 tablespoons fresh lime juice

1 teaspoon grated lime zest

1 pineapple, cut into bite-sized pieces

3 bananas, cut into bite-sized pieces

2 pints strawberries, washed and
    hulled

Wooden skewers

1. In a small bowl, combine sour cream, sugar, lime juice, and zest; stir until sugar is dissolved. Cover and refrigerate until serving time. (Can be made ahead, covered, and refrigerated up to 2 days.)

2. Just before serving, thread fruit on wooden skewers and arrange on a platter with the bowl of citrus cream in the center.

Honeyed Fruit Dip

The flavor of this dip changes depending on the honey that you use: clover honey is mild; buckwheat more robust.

PREP TIME: 10 MINUTES • MAKES: 1 ½ CUPS

1 package (8 ounces) cream cheese,
    softened
½ cup honey
1 teaspoon ground cinnamon
1 teaspoon vanilla extract
Fruit, cut into bite-sized pieces,
    for serving

In a small bowl, combine all ingredients except the fruit; stir until smooth. Cover and refrigerate 2 hours before serving. Serve with fruit.

Bar Food

Cheese Twists

Frozen puff pastry is wonderfully easy to use. You can also make these twists with jalapeño Jack or Romano cheese—just use the same amount.

PREP TIME: 20 MINUTES • BAKE TIME: 15 MINUTES • MAKES: ABOUT 28

½ package (17.3 ounces) frozen puff
   pastry sheets, thawed
1 large egg, beaten with 1 tablespoon
   water
¾ cup crumbled feta cheese with basil
   and tomato

1. Line a baking sheet with parchment; set aside. Unfold puff pastry on a lightly floured surface and roll into a 14-by-10-inch rectangle. Cut pastry in half lengthwise.

2. Brush pastry with egg mixture. Sprinkle cheese evenly over one pastry half. Lay the other pastry half, egg-side down, over the cheese-topped half. Roll gently with a rolling pin to press together.

3. With a pizza wheel, cut pastry crosswise into 28 half-inch-wide strips. Twist strips four or five times and place on a parchment-lined baking sheet, pressing the ends down. Brush strips with egg mixture. Refrigerate for 30 minutes.

4. Heat oven to 400°F. Bake 12 to 15 minutes until golden. Serve warm or at room temperature. (Store in an airtight container up to 3 days. Reheat in 400°F oven for 8 minutes to crisp.)

VARIATION

Havarti-Caraway Twists
Substitute ¾ cup shredded Havarti with caraway and ¼ cup chopped parsley for the feta.

Parmesan Crisps

In Italy, these are called "frici," which means "little trifles." Perfect for serving with a Caesar salad, they are traditionally made with montasio cheese, which can be difficult to find. We've used Parmesan instead.

PREP TIME: 10 MINUTES • BAKE TIME: 8 MINUTES • MAKES: ABOUT 12

1 cup shredded Parmesan cheese

1. Heat oven to 350°F. Line a baking sheet with parchment or silicone baking liner. Drop shredded cheese by table-spoons about 4 inches apart onto prepared baking sheet.

2. Bake until edges of cheese just begin to color. Cool on baking sheet. Serve immediately.

VARIATIONS

Asiago-Basil Crisps
Substitute 1 cup shredded asiago cheese for the Parmesan and toss the cheese with ½ teaspoon dried basil.

Cheddar Crisps
Substitute 1 cup shredded aged Cheddar for the Parmesan cheese.

Sweet and Hot Cashews

This recipe calls for raw cashews, which are usually found in health food stores. These taste better if made a day ahead.

PREP TIME: 10 MINUTES • **BAKE TIME: 15 MINUTES** • **MAKES: 3 CUPS**

1 large egg white, beaten
1 ½ teaspoons ground ginger
½ teaspoon kosher salt
½ teaspoon wasabi powder
3 cups raw cashews
⅓ cup sugar

1. Heat oven to 400°F. Lightly oil a nonstick baking sheet.

2. In a large bowl, beat the egg white, ginger, salt, and wasabi powder with a wire whisk. Add the cashews and toss until nuts are coated. Sprinkle on the sugar and toss again.

3. Spread the nuts in a single layer on the prepared pan. Bake 7 minutes. Remove pan from oven and stir nuts with a silicone spatula. Return pan to oven and continue baking for 8 more minutes. Cool on pan. (Cover and store in an airtight container up to 2 weeks.)

Barbecued Pecans

Make this recipe at least a day ahead—the nuts are soggy just after cooking, but they're crunchy after 24 hours.

PREP TIME: 5 MINUTES • BAKE TIME: 15 MINUTES • MAKES: 4 CUPS

2 tablespoons butter
¼ cup Worcestershire sauce
1 tablespoon ketchup
½ teaspoon soy sauce
½ teaspoon bottled hot pepper sauce
4 cups pecan halves
¾ teaspoon kosher salt

1. Heat oven to 375°F. In a large microwave-proof bowl, combine butter, Worcestershire sauce, ketchup, soy sauce, and hot pepper sauce. Cover and microwave for 1 minute. Stir to combine. Add nuts and toss until well coated.

2. Spread nuts in a single layer on an ungreased large baking sheet and bake for 15 minutes, stirring once. Remove pan to a wire rack and sprinkle with salt. Cool completely on pan. Store, covered, for 24 hours before serving. (Can be stored in an airtight container up to 2 weeks. If nuts get soggy, bake in a 375°F oven for 10 minutes to recrisp.)

VARIATION

Barbecued Almonds
Substitute 4 cups whole raw almonds for the pecans.

Spiced Walnuts

Boiling the walnuts before baking them is the key to these sweet-tasting nibbles. These taste better if made at least a day ahead.

PREP TIME: 10 MINUTES • **BAKE TIME: 30 MINUTES** • **MAKES: 3 CUPS**

½ cup sugar
¾ teaspoon crushed red pepper
½ teaspoon kosher salt
4 cups water
3 cups walnut halves

1. Heat oven to 400°F. Lightly grease a baking sheet. In a small bowl, combine the sugar, pepper, and salt.

2. Bring water to a boil. Add walnuts. Cover and cook for 5 minutes; drain. Return walnuts to saucepan and toss with sugar mixture until well coated.

3. Spread nuts in a single layer on prepared baking sheet. Bake 30 minutes. Cool completely on pan on a wire rack. Store nuts in an airtight container.

Potato-Caviar Bites

Buy the smallest new potatoes you can find; they are easier to pop into your mouth.

PREP TIME: 5 MINUTES • COOK TIME: 20 MINUTES • MAKES: ABOUT 48

24 very small new potatoes (about
   1 pound)
1 teaspoon salt
½ cup sour cream
½ teaspoon grated lemon zest
Dash freshly ground pepper
4 tablespoons lumpfish or salmon
   caviar

1. Place potatoes, salt, and cold water to cover in a large saucepan; cover and cook 10 to 15 minutes or until potatoes are fork-tender. Drain. When potatoes are cool enough to handle, cut in half.

2. In a small bowl, combine sour cream, lemon zest, and pepper. Place potatoes on serving platter; keep warm. To serve, spread ½ teaspoon sour cream on cut side of each potato; top each with ¼ teaspoon caviar.

Deviled Eggs

If you have any eggs left after the party, chop them and make egg salad.

PREP TIME: 20 MINUTES • **COOK TIME: 15 MINUTES** • **MAKES: 24**

12 large eggs
½ cup mayonnaise
2 tablespoons sour cream
2 teaspoons Dijon mustard
¼ teaspoon salt
Freshly ground pepper
Paprika, for garnish

1. Place eggs in a single layer in large saucepan. Add enough cold water to cover the eggs by 1 inch. Bring just to a boil over high heat. Cover and remove from heat. Let stand for 13 minutes. Pour off water and run eggs under cold water until cool enough to handle. Peel.

2. Cut eggs in half lengthwise and remove the yolks. In a small bowl, mash yolks with a fork until evenly crumbled.

Add mayonnaise, sour cream, mustard, salt, and pepper; stir until smooth. Spoon yolk mixture into egg white halves. Garnish with paprika. Refrigerate until ready to serve.

VARIATION

Curried Eggs
Omit Dijon mustard and add 1 teaspoon toasted curry powder to yolk mixture. (To toast curry powder, place in a small skillet and heat over medium heat 2 to 3 minutes until aromatic.)

Bacon-Spinach Deviled Eggs
Add 2 tablespoons chopped fresh spinach and 2 tablespoons crumbled cooked bacon to yolk mixture.

Marinated Olives

In addition to making great appetizers, these are a great hostess gift.

PREP TIME: 10 MINUTES (PLUS MARINATING) • MAKES: ABOUT 3 CUPS

1 pound kalamata olives
¼ cup olive oil
2 teaspoons chopped garlic
1 teaspoon minced fresh rosemary
    or thyme
1 teaspoon fennel seeds
½ teaspoon crushed red pepper
1 bay leaf

1. Crush the olives slightly with the side of a chef's knife.

2. Combine remaining ingredients in a large bowl. Add olives and toss. Cover and refrigerate at least 24 hours before serving, stirring occasionally. Bring to room temperature before serving. Remove bay leaf. Spoon into a serving bowl or sterilized decorative jar.

Basil Onion Rings

Any sweet onion will work for this recipe: Vidalia, Maui, Texas Sweets, or Walla Walla.

PREP TIME: 15 MINUTES • COOK TIME: 3 MINUTES PER BATCH • MAKES: 6 SERVINGS

8 cups vegetable oil for frying
1 large sweet onion, about 1 pound
½ cup milk
1 cup flour
1 tablespoon salt
1 teaspoon dried basil

1. In a deep-fat fryer or large deep saucepan, heat oil to 375°F on a deep-fat thermometer.

2. Slice onion into ¼-inch-thick rounds. Separate into rings. Place them in a large bowl, add milk, and toss to moisten.

3. In a medium bowl, combine flour, salt, and basil. Stir with a fork to mix.

4. Remove onions from milk; drain. Toss in flour. Then return to milk and toss again in flour. Fry a few pieces at a time for 2 to 3 minutes. Remove with slotted spoon and drain on paper towels. Repeat process, cooking all the onions.

VARIATIONS

Tex-Mex Onion Rings
Omit the basil and add 2 teaspoons chili powder and 1 teaspoon oregano to flour.

Curry Onion Rings
Omit the basil and add 2 teaspoons curry powder to flour.

Calamari

For tender results, cook less than one minute. This is great fast food!

PREP TIME: 20 MINUTES • **COOK TIME: 1 MINUTE PER BATCH** • **MAKES: 8 SERVINGS**

8 cups vegetable oil for frying
⅔ cup all-purpose flour
¼ teaspoon salt
⅓ cup beer
1 egg yolk
2 teaspoons olive oil
1 pound cleaned raw calamari, sliced
   into rings
Prepared tartar sauce or marinara
   sauce, for dipping

1. In a deep-fat fryer or large deep saucepan, heat vegetable oil to 375°F on a deep-fat thermometer.

2. In a medium bowl, combine flour and salt. Add beer, egg yolk, and olive oil and stir until smooth.

3. Dip calamari into batter, a few pieces at a time. Carefully place in hot oil and cook 1 minute. Remove with a slotted spoon to paper towels to drain; sprinkle with salt. Keep warm in 200°F oven until ready to serve. Repeat with remaining calamari. Serve warm with your favorite tartar sauce or heated marinara sauce.

Fried Mozzarella

The coated cheese is "fried" in the oven. Serve with your favorite marinara sauce.

PREP TIME: 45 MINUTES • **BAKE TIME: 8 MINUTES** • **MAKES: 12 STICKS**

1 package (9 ounces) mozzarella
   cheese sticks
1 cup plain dried bread crumbs
⅓ cup all-purpose flour
2 large eggs, beaten
¾ cup marinara sauce

1. Remove cheese from wrappers. Place bread crumbs, flour, and eggs in three individual bowls. Dip a cheese stick in eggs, then flour, then eggs again, and last in crumbs. Place on greased baking sheet. Repeat with remaining cheese sticks.

2. Refrigerate breaded cheese sticks for 30 minutes.

3. Heat oven to 375°F. Bake cheese sticks for 8 minutes. Warm marinara sauce before serving as a dip.

Potato Skins

To save time, bake the potatoes in the microwave but rotate them once during cooking.

PREP TIME: 30 MINUTES • BAKE TIME: 15 MINUTES • MAKES: 20

5 large baking potatoes
1 tablespoon olive oil
¼ teaspoon bottled red pepper sauce
1 package (8 ounces) shredded
  Mexican-style cheese (Cheddar,
  Jack, asadero, and queso blanco)
6 slices precooked bacon, chopped
¼ cup chopped green onions
¼ cup chopped pickled jalapeño
  peppers
½ cup sour cream
1 tablespoon red wine vinegar
2 teaspoons snipped fresh chives

1. Scrub the potatoes and prick all over with a fork. Cook in the microwave on 100% power 15 to 20 minutes, turning potatoes once during cooking. Let cool.

2. Cut each potato lengthwise into four wedges. Carefully scoop out the inside of each potato with a teaspoon, leaving a ¼-inch shell. Reserve 1½ cups potato pulp and cut into cubes.

3. Heat oven to 425°F. In a small cup, combine oil and pepper sauce. With a pastry brush, brush the insides of the potato skins with the oil mixture and place on a baking sheet. In a bowl, toss potato cubes, cheese, bacon, green onions, and peppers. Spoon filling into the potato skins.

4. Bake for 15 minutes until potato skins are heated through and cheese has melted. In a medium bowl, combine sour cream, vinegar, and chives. Serve potato skins with sour cream dip.

Chicken Satay

Soak wooden skewers in water for at least 15 minutes before use to keep them from burning under the broiler.

PREP TIME: 20 MINUTES • **BROIL TIME: 6 MINUTES** • **MAKES: ABOUT 24**

1 pound skinless, boneless chicken
    breasts (about 3 half breasts)
½ cup bottled ginger and garlic
    marinade
1 tablespoon peanut butter
1 tablespoon lemon juice
Wooden skewers

1. Place the chicken in the freezer for 30 minutes for easier slicing.

2. Cut chicken into ½-inch-thick slices. In a glass dish, combine the marinade, peanut butter, and lemon juice. Add chicken and toss to coat. Cover and marinate for 1 or up to 24 hours.

3. Heat broiler. Thread one piece of chicken onto each skewer and place on a baking sheet. Broil 6 minutes, turning once. Serve immediately.

VARIATION

Beef Satay
Substitute 1 pound flank or top round steak for chicken. For easier slicing, freeze meat for 45 minutes; slice meat into ¾-inch-thick slices. Prepare marinade and add the beef. Continue marinating and cooking as above.

Pot Stickers

Wonton wrappers are found in the Asian section of the supermarket.

PREP TIME: 20 MINUTES • COOK TIME: 12 MINUTES PER BATCH • MAKES: 36

1 cup ground pork

1 ½ teaspoons grated fresh ginger

2 tablespoons soy sauce, plus
    additional for serving

¼ cup chopped water chestnuts

2 tablespoons chopped green onions

36 wonton wrappers

4 tablespoons vegetable oil, divided

1. Combine the pork with the ginger, 2 tablespoons soy sauce, water chestnuts, and green onions in a small bowl and mix well. Spoon a teaspoon of filling in the center of a wonton wrapper. Moisten edge of wonton with water. Fold wonton over filling and pinch to seal. Keep filled wontons covered with a damp paper towel while preparing remainder.

2. In a large skillet, heat 2 tablespoons oil. Add about half of the dumplings—do not crowd the pan. Cover and cook over medium-low heat 5 minutes. Add ¾ cup water to skillet; cover and cook 3 minutes. Then uncover and cook 3 more minutes until water is evaporated. Repeat with remaining dumplings and oil. Serve with soy sauce.

Hot Chile Quesadillas

Any shredded cheese will work but the Mexican-style four cheeses is my first choice.

PREP TIME: 15 MINUTES • COOK TIME: 4 MINUTES PER BATCH • MAKES: 40

1 package (11.5 ounces) flour
   tortillas, 10 count
2 cups shredded Mexican-style cheese
   (Cheddar, Jack, asadero, and queso
   blanco)
2 cans (4 ounces each) chopped green
   chiles, drained
Ground cumin to taste
Prepared salsa and sour cream, for
   serving

1. Lay a tortilla on a work surface and cover it with ¼ cup cheese, 1 table-spoon of the chiles, and a dash of cumin. Lightly moisten another tortilla with water and place, water-side down, over cheese. Repeat, making 4 more quesadillas with remaining tortillas, cheese, chilis, and cumin.

2. Spray a large skillet with nonstick cooking spray and heat over medium heat. Arrange 2 quesadillas in the skillet and cook for 2 minutes; turn and cook on the other side. Keep warm in a 200°F oven until ready to serve. Repeat with remaining quesadillas.

3. Using kitchen scissors, cut each quesadilla into 8 wedges. Serve with salsa and sour cream.

VARIATION

Chorizo-Cheese Quesadillas
Omit green chiles and cumin. Top each tortilla with 1 tablespoon cooked diced chorizo sausage and ½ tablespoon chopped cilantro.

Spring Rolls

No cooking required for these Asian-inspired shrimp and vegetable rolls.

PREP TIME: 20 MINUTES • MAKES: 4 ROLLS

4 sheets rice paper (available in the
   Asian foods section)
12 cooked, shelled, and deveined
   shrimp, halved lengthwise
1 cup shredded carrots
1 cup fresh bean sprouts
2 green onions, cut into 4-inch lengths
1 tablespoon finely chopped peanuts,
   optional
Fresh mint leaves
Fresh basil or cilantro leaves
Bottled teriyaki sauce, for dipping

1. Assemble all the ingredients; set aside.

2. Place one sheet of rice paper in a bowl of warm water (110 to 120°F) for 10 seconds. It will continue to soften as you work with it. Carefully transfer to a clean linen towel.

3. Arrange 6 shrimp halves in the middle of the paper and pile one-quarter of all the ingredients, except teriyaki sauce, on top. Roll up, folding in the ends burrito-style, as tightly as you can. Repeat with remaining ingredients and rice paper. Serve at room temperature with teriyaki sauce.

Irish Nachos

Potatoes are the base for this fun party food.

PREP TIME: 10 MINUTES • **BROIL TIME: 2 MINUTES** • **MAKES: 4 SERVINGS**

1 package (16 ounces) frozen oven
fries with sea salt and olive oil
(about 2 ½ cups)
1 ½ cups shredded Mexican-style
cheese (Cheddar and Monterey
Jack)
2 tablespoons canned chopped green
chiles
½ cup prepared salsa
3 tablespoons chopped fresh cilantro

1. Place potatoes on a foil-lined baking sheet and bake according to package directions, turning once. Remove from oven and heat broiler.

2. Sprinkle cheese and chiles over the cooked potatoes. Return to oven and broil until cheese melts.

3. Combine the salsa and cilantro. Spoon over the nachos and serve immediately.

Original Nachos

Small round tortilla chips work best for this dish. You choose how much heat you want in the salsa.

PREP TIME: 10 MINUTES • BROIL TIME: 2 MINUTES • MAKES: 6 SERVINGS

8 cups tortilla chips

1 ½ cups shredded Mexican-style four-cheese mix (Cheddar, Jack, queso blanco, and asadero)

2 tablespoons canned chopped green chiles

½ cup prepared salsa

1 tablespoon chopped fresh cilantro

1. Heat broiler. In a 9½-inch metal tart or cake pan with a removable bottom, place half the tortilla chips. Sprinkle half the cheese over the chips, then half the chiles; top with remaining chips, cheese, and chiles.

2. Place the pan on a baking sheet. Broil, 10 inches from heat source, for 2 minutes until cheese melts and is bubbly.

3. Remove bottom from pan and place on a serving plate. Combine the salsa and cilantro. Spoon over nachos and serve immediately.

VARIATION

Beef or Chicken Nachos

Add ½ pound precooked shredded beef or chicken and toss with the chiles. Continue preparing nachos as above.

Shrimp Quesadillas

Scissors are the perfect kitchen gadget for cutting the quesadillas into wedges.

PREP TIME: 20 MINUTES • COOK TIME: 4 MINUTES PER BATCH • MAKES: 30

½ cup prepared salsa, plus additional
    for serving
1 package (11.5 ounces) flour
    tortillas, about 7 inches
2 cups shredded Mexican-style four-
    cheese mix (Cheddar, Jack,
    asadero, and queso blanco)
½ pound cooked, shelled, and
    deveined shrimp, finely chopped
¼ cup chopped fresh cilantro
½ cup sour cream
1½ teaspoons grated lemon zest

1. Lay a tortilla on a work surface. Spread it with 1 tablespoon salsa, then add ¼ cup cheese, ¼ cup shrimp, and a sprinkle of cilantro. Lightly moisten another tortilla with water and place, water-side down, over the filling. Repeat, making 4 more quesadillas with remaining tortillas, salsa, cheese, shrimp, and cilantro.

2. Combine sour cream and lemon zest in a small bowl; set aside. Spray a large skillet with nonstick cooking spray and heat over medium heat. Cook quesadilla in skillet 2 minutes, turn, and cook 2 more minutes on the other side. Keep warm in a 200°F oven until ready to serve. Repeat with remaining quesadillas.

3. Using kitchen scissors, cut each quesadilla into 6 wedges. Serve warm with lemon cream and additional salsa.

Chinese Chicken Wings

These wings roast in a rich broth to a deep mahogany color.

PREP TIME: 15 MINUTES • **ROAST TIME: 60 MINUTES** • **MAKES: ABOUT 24**

3 pounds chicken wings
1 cup soy sauce
½ cup sherry
½ cup firmly packed brown sugar
2 tablespoons finely chopped fresh
   ginger
2 teaspoons grated lime zest

1. Heat oven to 400°F. Cut off wing tips; discard. Cut each wing at its joint into 2 pieces. Rinse wings well and dry with paper towels.

2. Arrange wings in a large roasting pan. Combine remaining ingredients in a 1-quart measuring cup; stir until sugar dissolves. Pour over wings.

3. Roast 30 minutes. Turn wings and continue roasting for 20 more minutes. Carefully pour off drippings in pan. Bake 10 more minutes until wings reach a deep brown color. Serve hot.

Buffalo Chicken Wings

This is the quintessential Sunday-afternoon football-watching snack.

PREP TIME: 15 MINUTES • **BAKE TIME: 50 TO 55 MINUTES** • **MAKES: ABOUT 24**

3 pounds chicken wings
¼ cup bottled red pepper sauce
1 tablespoon bottled chipotle sauce
2 tablespoons butter, melted
½ cup bottled blue cheese salad
    dressing, for serving
Celery sticks, for garnish

1. Heat oven to 400°F. Line a 15½ x 10 x 1-inch jelly roll pan with foil; set aside.

2. Cut off wing tips; discard. Cut each wing at its joint into 2 pieces. Rinse wings well and dry with paper towels. Arrange wings in a single layer on prepared pan. Bake 30 minutes.

3. In a small bowl, combine the sauces and butter. Remove baking pan from oven. Drain off drippings from the wings. Brush wings with half the butter mixture. Bake 10 minutes. Turn wings and brush with remaining butter mixture. Return to oven and bake 10 more minutes. Serve wings with blue cheese dressing and celery sticks.

Chinese Baby Back Ribs

Start with cooked baby back pork ribs—it cuts the time by three hours.

PREP TIME: 15 MINUTES • BAKE TIME: 40 MINUTES • MAKES: 12 TO 14 RIBS

1 package (34.4 ounces) fully cooked
    baby back pork ribs
½ cup soy sauce
3 tablespoons finely chopped fresh
    ginger
1 teaspoon Asian sesame oil
1 teaspoon five-spice powder

1. Heat oven to 375°F. Line a roasting pan with foil; set aside.

2. Remove ribs from package. Wipe off the sauce and discard. Rinse ribs under warm water; pat dry with paper towels (some sauce will remain). Arrange ribs in a single layer in prepared pan.

3. In a small bowl, combine soy sauce, ginger, and sesame oil; stir until well mixed. Pour over ribs. Cover pan with foil. Bake for 35 minutes.

4. Remove ribs from oven; carefully remove foil from pan. Sprinkle ribs with five-spice powder. Return to oven and continue baking, uncovered, for 5 more minutes. To serve, cut each rack into individual ribs.

Texas Barbecue Ribs

Ribs in Texas means beef. The ribs are rubbed with a dry spice before baking.

PREP TIME: 10 MINUTES • **BAKE TIME: 55 MINUTES** • **MAKES: 8 OR 9 RIBS**

1 package (32 ounces) fully cooked
    split beef back ribs
2 tablespoons dried barbecue
    seasoning

1. Heat oven to 375°F. Line a roasting pan with foil; set aside.

2. Remove ribs from package. Wipe off the sauce and discard. Rinse ribs under warm water; pat dry with paper towels (some sauce will remain). Arrange ribs in a single layer in prepared pan and sprinkle with seasoning.

3. Cover pan with foil and and bake for 50 minutes. Carefully remove foil from pan and continue baking, uncovered, for 5 more minutes. To serve, cut each rack into individual ribs. Serve warm.

Pizza Margherita

This is a "white pizza," meaning no tomato sauce on the crust.

PREP TIME: 10 MINUTES • BAKE TIME: 8 TO 10 MINUTES • MAKES: 16 PIECES

1 package (10 ounces) small baked pizza crusts

1 package (8 ounces) shredded mozzarella cheese

1 large (8-ounce) fresh tomato, chopped

¼ cup julienned fresh basil leaves

1. Heat oven to 450°F. Remove crusts from wrappers and place on an ungreased baking sheet.

2. For each pizza, sprinkle 1 cup cheese on the crust, then half the tomato, and top with half the basil.

3. Bake for 8 to 10 minutes until cheese is bubbly. Let pizzas cool slightly, transfer to a cutting board, and, using a pizza wheel, cut each pizza into 8 wedges.

Sausage and Salami Pizza

Salami on pizza? Try it. You'll be pleasantly surprised.

PREP TIME: 20 MINUTES • BAKE TIME: 8 TO 10 MINUTES • MAKES: 16 PIECES

1 package (10 ounces) small baked
    pizza crusts
1 cup shredded mozzarella cheese
½ cup cooked and crumbled sweet
    Italian sausage (about ¼ pound
    raw; remove from casing if in links)
8 slices sopressata salami, each slice
    cut in half
½ cup ricotta cheese
Freshly ground pepper

1. Heat oven to 450°F. Remove crusts from wrappers and place on an ungreased baking sheet.

2. For each pizza, sprinkle ½ cup mozzarella on the crust. Top with half the crumbled sausage and salami. Spoon dollops of ricotta cheese over both. Season with pepper.

3. Bake for 8 to 10 minutes until cheese is bubbly. Let pizzas cool slightly, transfer to a cutting board, and, using a pizza wheel, cut each pizza into 8 wedges.

VARIATION

Roasted Pepper and Sausage Pizza
Omit the ricotta cheese and salami. Spread each crust with ¼ cup bottled pizza sauce and half the crumbled sausage. Top each pizza with 1 tablespoon chopped roasted red pepper. Bake as directed above.

Vegetarian Pizza

The packaged sliced mushrooms are a real time-saver.

PREP TIME: 20 MINUTES • BAKE TIME: 8 TO 10 MINUTES • MAKES: 16 PIECES

1 package (10 ounces) small baked
   pizza crusts
½ cup bottled pizza sauce
1 tablespoon olive oil
1 small onion, halved and sliced
1 package (4 ounces) sliced cremini
   mushrooms
⅛ teaspoon kosher salt
About ½ cup baby spinach leaves
1 cup shredded mozzarella cheese
   (4 ounces)

1. Heat oven to 450°F. Remove crusts from wrappers and place on an ungreased baking sheet. Spread pizza sauce evenly on each crust.

2. Heat oil in a large skillet for 1 minute. Add onion and mushrooms and cook for 3 to 5 minutes, stirring frequently, until onion is soft and mushrooms have browned. Sprinkle with salt. Divide the mushroom mixture evenly and spread over the pizza sauce. Add spinach; top with cheese.

3. Bake for 8 to 10 minutes until cheese is bubbly. Let cool slightly, transfer to a cutting board, and, using a pizza wheel, cut each pizza into 8 wedges.

VARIATION

Wild Mushroom Pizza
Substitute one package (8 ounces) sliced exotic mushrooms for the creminis. Bake as directed above.

Smoked Salmon Pizza

No need to knead bread dough. Use flour tortillas for the crust for this "pizza."

PREP TIME: 10 MINUTES • COOK TIME: 10 MINUTES • MAKES: 24

1 teaspoon vegetable oil
4 flour tortillas, about 7 inches
4 tablespoons chive-and-onion cream
   cheese
1 package (4 ounces) sliced smoked
   salmon
Freshly ground pepper
Lemon juice
Fresh dill sprigs, for garnish

1. Heat oven to 200°F. In a large skillet, heat the oil. Add one tortilla and cook for 2 minutes, turning once. Keep tortilla warm in oven while cooking remainder.

2. Spread cream cheese evenly over tortillas; arrange smoked salmon evenly on top. Sprinkle with pepper and lemon juice; garnish with dill. Using kitchen scissors, cut each pizza into 6 wedges. Serve immediately.

Caponata

This Sicilian dish is best served at room temperature.

PREP TIME: 20 MINUTES • COOK TIME: 30 MINUTES • MAKES: 2½ CUPS

1 tablespoon olive oil
1 medium onion, chopped
1 celery rib, finely chopped
1 pound eggplant (preferably 2 small),
    peeled and cut into ½-inch cubes
⅓ cup bottled roasted red peppers
¼ cup mild sweet piquant peppers
1 can (14.5 ounces) diced tomatoes
    with garlic and olive oil
1 teaspoon dried basil
2 tablespoons drained capers
Salt and pepper
Toasted bread slices, for serving

1. In a large skillet, heat olive oil. Add onion and celery and cook until soft, 2 minutes. Add eggplant and stir to coat; cover and cook 10 minutes.

2. Add remaining ingredients except capers and salt and pepper; continue cooking, covered, 20 more minutes, stirring occasionally.

3. Spoon into a bowl and cool. Cover and refrigerate up to 24 hours. Stir in capers. Taste and season with salt and pepper, if needed. Serve with toasted bread slices.

Salsa Cruda

Rinsing the raw onions in hot water removes any bitterness.

PREP TIME: 10 MINUTES • MAKES: 1 ½ CUPS

½ medium onion, minced (½ cup)
1 large tomato, seeded and chopped
1 tablespoon fresh lime juice
½ teaspoon bottled chipotle sauce
½ teaspoon salt
2 tablespoons chopped cilantro
Tortilla chips, for serving

1. Place the onion in a medium bowl. Pour on hot tap water and let stand for 4 minutes. Drain well.

2. Return onion to bowl and add remaining ingredients except tortilla chips; stir well. Serve with tortilla chips.

VARIATION

Jícama Salsa Cruda
Add ½ cup peeled and diced fresh jícama.

Shrimp Salsa Cruda
Add ½ cup chopped shelled and deveined cooked shrimp.

Just One Bite

Sun-Dried Tomato Puffs

When made in the usual large ring, this dish is called a gougère. But when dropped by teaspoonfuls, it is perfect for one-bite fare.

PREP TIME: 20 MINUTES • **BAKE TIME: 20 TO 25 MINUTES** • **MAKES: ABOUT 40**

½ cup water
½ stick (¼ cup) butter
½ cup all-purpose flour
1 tablespoon minced oil-packed
    sun-dried tomatoes
½ teaspoon dried basil
2 large eggs
¼ cup grated Parmesan cheese

1. Heat oven to 375°F. In a small saucepan, bring water and butter to a full boil over medium heat. Add the flour and stir with a wooden spoon until mixture pulls away from the sides of the pan. Stir in tomatoes and basil. Let cool for 5 minutes, stirring occasionally. Add eggs, one at a time, beating after each addition, until the batter is stiff and smooth. Stir in the cheese.

2. Grease a large baking sheet. Spoon batter by teaspoonfuls 1 inch apart onto prepared baking sheet. Bake 20 to 25 minutes until puffed and firm to the touch.

VARIATIONS

Cheddar Puffs
Prepare and bake as above but omit tomatoes, basil, and Parmesan cheese and add ½ cup shredded Cheddar cheese.

Goat Cheese Puffs
Prepare and bake as above but omit tomatoes, basil, and Parmesan cheese. Add ½ teaspoon oregano and ¼ cup crumbled goat cheese.

Cheese Puffs

There are just three ingredients in these can't-eat-just-one appetizers. Use bulk sausage, the hotter the better.

PREP TIME: 30 MINUTES • BAKE TIME: 20 MINUTES PER BATCH • MAKES: 60

1 package (12 ounces) hot bulk pork
    sausage
1 package (8 ounces) shredded
    Cheddar cheese
2½ cups all-purpose baking mix

1. Heat oven to 350°F. In a medium bowl, combine all ingredients; mix well.

2. Roll mixture into 1-inch balls and place one inch apart on ungreased baking sheets. Bake until golden, about 20 minutes. Serve warm. (Can be made ahead, cooled, covered, and stored in freezerproof containers. Freeze up to 1 month. Reheat in a 350°F oven for 8 minutes.)

Cheese Wafers

Want more heat? Just add a half teaspoon more of cayenne pepper.

PREP TIME: 10 MINUTES PLUS CHILLING • **BAKE TIME: 20 MINUTES** • **MAKES: 72**

2 cups grated sharp Cheddar cheese
   (8 ounces)
6 to 8 tablespoons butter, melted
1 cup self-rising flour
½ teaspoon ground cayenne pepper

1. In a large bowl, combine cheese and 6 tablespoons melted butter. Beat with an electric mixer on low speed until well combined.

2. In a medium bowl, combine flour and pepper. Stir with a whisk until well combined. Stir flour into cheese mixture, adding more melted butter if needed, until pastry begins to hold together. Divide in half. Shape pastry into two 12-inch logs, 1 inch in diameter. Wrap each log in wax paper and refrigerate until firm, at least 1 hour or overnight.

3. Heat oven to 350°F. Cut each log into ¼-inch-thick slices. Arrange slices on two ungreased baking sheets. Bake until golden, 18 to 20 minutes. (Can be made ahead. Freeze baked wafers in an airtight container up to 1 month. Thaw at room temperature.)

VARIATION

Basil Cheese Wafers
Prepare as above, using only 6 tablespoons butter and reducing the cayenne pepper to ¼ teaspoon. Add 2 tablespoons prepared basil pesto to the butter-cheese mixture. Shape, refrigerate, and bake as directed above.

Crispy Cheddar Bites

Added to these Cheddar cheese crisps, toasted-rice cereal contributes crunch and texture. This is a great do-ahead recipe: make and shape the dough in advance, but bake the day of the party.

PREP TIME: 20 MINUTES • BAKE TIME: 10 TO 12 MINUTES • MAKES: ABOUT 50

1 stick (½ cup) butter, softened
2½ cups (20 ounces) shredded
   Cheddar cheese
1 cup all-purpose flour
½ teaspoon garlic salt
½ teaspoon dried basil
1 cup toasted rice cereal

1. In a large bowl, beat butter with an electric mixer on low speed until creamy. Add the cheese and continue beating until well mixed. Add the flour, garlic salt, and basil. Beat on low speed until incorporated. Stir in the cereal. The dough may be crumbly. Knead until dough holds together.

2. Divide dough in half. On a sheet of wax paper, form dough into a 10-inch log. Wrap and refrigerate until firm. Repeat with remaining dough.

3. Heat oven to 350°F. Cut rolls into ¼-inch slices. Place on ungreased baking sheets. Bake one sheet at a time 10 to 12 minutes. Serve at room temperature.

Potato Latkes

This version is made in a mini size but topped with the usual applesauce and sour cream. Latkes are also wonderful topped with smoked salmon or caviar.

PREP TIME: 10 MINUTES • COOK TIME: 5 MINUTES PER BATCH • MAKES: ABOUT 40

3½ cups refrigerated shredded
   potatoes, divided
1 small onion, chopped (about ½ cup)
⅓ cup boiling water
⅓ cup matzo meal
2 large eggs, beaten
½ teaspoon baking powder
½ teaspoon salt
2 tablespoons vegetable oil
Applesauce and sour cream, for
   serving

1. Place 1½ cups shredded potatoes and the onion into the bowl of a food processor with the steel blade attached. Pulse just until coarsely chopped.

Transfer mixture to a medium bowl. Pour hot water over the mixture and stir well.

2. Add the matzo meal, eggs, baking powder, and salt to potato-onion mixture; stir to combine. Fold in reserved 2 cups potatoes.

3. Heat oven to 200°F. In a large skillet, heat oil over medium-high heat. Drop batter by teaspoonfuls into hot skillet. Cook until golden brown, turn, and cook other side. Keep warm in oven while cooking remaining batter. (Can be made ahead. Cool to room temperature, cover, and refrigerate up to 2 days. Reheat in a 375°F oven for 8 minutes.) Serve with applesauce and sour cream on the side.

Classic Mini Quiches

Some things just can't be improved upon and Quiche Lorraine is one of them.

PREP TIME: 20 MINUTES • **BAKE TIME: 10 MINUTES** • **MAKES: 45**

1 tablespoon butter or margarine

½ cup chopped green onions

4 large eggs

1 cup heavy cream

Dash freshly ground pepper

Dash nutmeg

3 packages (2.1 ounces each) mini
    phyllo dough shells

6 slices precooked bacon, crumbled

1 cup (4 ounces) shredded Swiss or
    Cheddar cheese

1. Heat oven to 425°F. In a medium skillet, melt the butter. Add the green onions; cook until onions are tender, about 3 to 5 minutes.

2. In a medium bowl, beat eggs with a wire whisk until smooth. Add the heavy cream and whisk until smooth. Add cooked green onions, pepper, and nutmeg; stir.

3. Arrange dough shells on ungreased baking sheets. Spoon ½ teaspoon each cooked bacon and shredded cheese into the shells. Fill with the egg mixture. Bake until filling is firm, about 10 minutes. (Can be made ahead, cooled, covered, and frozen up to 2 weeks. Thaw and then reheat in a 425°F oven for 8 minutes.) Serve warm.

Mini Spinach Quiches

A prepared spinach soufflé is the base for this quick one-bite quiche.

PREP TIME: 15 MINUTES • BAKE TIME: 15 MINUTES • MAKES: 30 SERVINGS

1 package (12 ounces) frozen spinach
    soufflé, thawed
⅓ cup grated Parmesan cheese
1 tablespoon chopped fresh dill
2 packages (2.1 ounces each) mini
    phyllo dough shells

1. Heat oven to 375°F. In a medium bowl, combine thawed spinach, cheese, and dill; stir to mix.

2. Arrange dough shells on ungreased baking sheets. Spoon spinach mixture evenly into the shells. Bake until filling is puffed, about 15 minutes. Serve warm. (Can be made ahead, cooled, covered, and refrigerated up to 2 days. Reheat in a 375°F oven for 10 minutes.)

VARIATION

Mini Ham and Spinach Quiches
Omit the fresh dill. Add ¼ cup finely chopped ham and reduce the Parmesan cheese to 3 tablespoons. Prepare and bake as directed above.

Mini Veggie Tortas

These are like little savory cheesecakes.

PREP TIME: **20 MINUTES** • BAKE TIME: **12 TO 15 MINUTES** • MAKES: **30**

1 container (8 ounces) garden
    vegetable cream cheese
1 large egg
¼ cup grated fresh Parmesan cheese
2 tablespoons chopped fresh basil
¼ teaspoon salt
Dash freshly ground pepper
2 packages (2.1 ounces each) baked
    mini phyllo dough shells

1. Heat oven to 375°F. In a medium bowl, stir cream cheese to soften. Add the egg and stir until well combined. Add the remaining ingredients except the phyllo shells and stir until well combined.

2. Arrange dough shells on ungreased baking sheets. Spoon the cheese mixture evenly into the shells. Bake until filling is firm, 12 to 15 minutes. (Can be made ahead, cooled, covered, and refrigerated up to 3 days. Reheat in a 375°F oven until heated through, about 8 minutes.) Serve warm.

Chicken-Pecan Tartlets

These tartlets have roots in the South. Pecans and chicken are a match made in heaven.

PREP TIME: 15 MINUTES • **BAKE TIME: 5 MINUTES** • **MAKES: 30**

2 packages (2.1 ounces each) baked
   mini phyllo dough shells
1 package (6 ounces) fully cooked
   chicken breast, finely chopped
3 tablespoons finely chopped pecans
3 tablespoons finely chopped celery
¼ cup mayonnaise

1. Heat oven to 350°F. Arrange dough shells on an ungreased baking sheet. Heat for 5 minutes until crisp. Cool.

2. In a medium bowl, combine the remaining ingredients and stir until well combined. (Can be made ahead, cooled, covered, and refrigerated up to 3 hours.) To serve, spoon the chicken mixture into the shells.

VARIATION

Curried Chicken Tartlets
Omit pecans. Substitute 3 tablespoons chopped apple and add ¼ teaspoon curry powder. Prepare and serve as above.

Sausage Pies

There are a variety of new sausage combinations on the market today—feel free to experiment with other flavors.

PREP TIME: 10 MINUTES • **BAKE TIME: 15 MINUTES** • **MAKES: 30**

1 chicken and apple sausage link
½ cup chive and onion cream cheese
1 tablespoon Dijon mustard
1 cup shredded Cheddar cheese
2 packages (2.1 ounces each) mini
   phyllo dough shells

1. Finely chop the sausage link. In a medium bowl, combine the cream cheese and mustard and stir to combine; add the sausage and the cheese and stir again until well mixed.

2. Heat oven to 375°F. Arrange dough shells on an ungreased baking sheet. Spoon sausage mixture evenly into the shells. (Can be made ahead, cooled, covered, and refrigerated up to 3 hours.) Bake 15 minutes. Serve warm.

Chicken Liver Tartlets

Chicken-liver lovers will eat these up.

PREP TIME: 25 MINUTES • BAKE TIME: 10 MINUTES PER BATCH • MAKES: 36

1 pound chicken livers
3 tablespoons butter
1 cup chopped onions
¼ cup red wine
1 teaspoon salt
⅛ teaspoon freshly ground pepper
36 puff pastry tartlet shells, thawed
    and baked according to package
    directions
2 tablespoons chopped parsley

1. Heat oven to 350°F. Rinse, drain, and trim the chicken livers, using kitchen scissors to snip away the connective tissue and fat. Chop the livers.

2. Melt butter in a large skillet. Add the onions and cook for 2 to 3 minutes to soften. Add the chicken livers and cook until they are no longer pink in the center. Add wine, salt, and pepper; cook 5 more minutes.

3. To serve, spoon chicken livers into baked pastry shells and garnish with chopped parsley.

Coconut-Chicken Bites

Once you've tasted these sweet and savory little bites, it will be hard to stop eating them!

PREP TIME: 15 MINUTES • BAKE TIME: 16 TO 18 MINUTES • MAKES: 36

1 ½ cups sweetened flaked coconut
1 pound boneless chicken tenders
⅓ cup plain yogurt or buttermilk
1 teaspoon salt
¼ teaspoon ground cayenne pepper
¾ cup packaged plain bread crumbs
1 bottle (5 ounces) duck sauce

1. Heat oven to 400°F. Spread coconut evenly on a nonstick baking sheet. Bake 6 to 8 minutes, stirring halfway through for even toasting. Remove from oven and cool. Keep oven on.

2. Cut the chicken into 1-inch chunks. In a medium bowl, combine yogurt or buttermilk, salt, and pepper; add chicken and toss to coat. Set aside.

3. Spoon the toasted coconut and bread crumbs into the bowl of a food processor with the steel blade attached. Pulse until coconut is ground. Pour crumb mixture into a sealable plastic bag. Add half the drained chicken, close the bag completely, and shake to coat. Remove chicken from bag and place on the nonstick baking sheet. Repeat, coating the remaining chicken. Bake until crisp, 10 to 12 minutes. Serve with duck sauce.

VARIATION

Coconut Shrimp Bites
Substitute 1 pound frozen medium cooked shelled and deveined shrimp, thawed, for the chicken. Prepare as above. Bake 8 to 10 minutes.

Mini Dog Bites

If you can't find cocktail franks, you can always cut regular hot dogs into one-inch bites.

PREP TIME: **5 MINUTES** • COOK TIME: **20 MINUTES** • MAKES: **30**

1 ½ cups bottled barbecue sauce
⅔ cup orange marmalade
½ teaspoon dry mustard
1 package (12 ounces) cocktail franks

1. In a large saucepan, combine the barbecue sauce, marmalade, and mustard. Cook over medium-high heat until bubbly, stirring occasionally. Add the franks.

2. Cover and reduce heat to medium and cook for 10 minutes, stirring occasionally. (Can be made ahead, covered, and refrigerated up to 3 days. Reheat over medium heat, about 5 minutes.) To serve, transfer to a small slow cooker or chafing dish to keep warm.

Rumaki

This classic appetizer can be assembled ahead of time and broiled just before serving.

PREP TIME: 15 MINUTES • **BROIL TIME: 8 MINUTES** • **MAKES: ABOUT 24**

¾ pound chicken livers (about 12)

⅔ cup teriyaki sauce

1 teaspoon chopped fresh garlic

12 to 14 slices bacon, cut in half, crosswise

1 can (8 ounces) sliced water chestnuts

1. Rinse, drain, and trim livers, using kitchen scissors to snip away connective tissue and fat. Cut each one in half; quarter any livers that are extra large. Place livers in a small bowl. Add teriyaki sauce and garlic. Cover and marinate in the refrigerator for 4 to 24 hours.

2. Drain livers. Lay the bacon out on a work surface. Top each piece with a chicken liver, then a water chestnut. Roll up the bacon and secure the package with a toothpick pierced through the overlapping ends and out the other side. Place on a broiler pan. Broil, 4 inches from heat source, 8 to 10 minutes until livers are no longer pink, turning once. Serve warm.

Angels on Horseback

Oysters are the traditional "angels" in this sinful hors d'oeuvre. The smaller size of center-cut bacon is just perfect for this recipe.

PREP TIME: 20 MINUTES • **BROIL TIME: 7 TO 9 MINUTES** • **MAKES: 40 TO 44**

1 pound large sea scallops (about 20 to 22)
¼ cup soy sauce
1 package (12 ounces) center-cut bacon
⅓ cup preserved ginger slices

1. Remove and discard the tough muscle attached to the scallop. Cut each scallop in half horizontally. Place scallops in a medium bowl and add soy sauce; toss to coat.

2. Heat broiler. Cut bacon in half crosswise. Place a scallop on one end of a bacon slice and top with a piece of ginger. Roll up and place on a broiler pan, with bacon ends tucked under.

3. Broil bacon-wrapped scallops until crisp and slightly browned, 4 to 5 minutes. Turn scallops and continue broiling 3 to 4 minutes more. Drain. Serve immediately with toothpicks.

VARIATION

Devils on Horseback
Omit soy sauce and ginger. Substitute 24 pitted prunes for the scallops and add 12 pimiento-stuffed green olives, halved. Place an olive half on a prune, wrap both in bacon, and secure with a toothpick. Repeat with remaining ingredients. Broil as directed above.

Cilantro Pesto Shrimp

For the holidays, make both the cilantro pesto and red pepper pesto recipes and serve together. The contrast of the red and green is very festive.

PREP TIME: 10 MINUTES • MAKES: 36 TO 40

1 pound frozen fully cooked shelled and deveined medium shrimp, thawed
¾ cup prepared basil pesto
½ cup fresh cilantro leaves
¼ teaspoon salt

1. Remove tails from shrimp, if they are attached. Place shrimp in a medium bowl.

2. In the bowl of a food processor with the steel blade attached, combine remaining ingredients. Pulse until well mixed. Pour mixture over the shrimp and toss until shrimp are well coated. (Can be made ahead, covered, and refrigerated up to 3 hours.) Serve with toothpicks.

VARIATION

Red Pepper Pesto
Prepare sauce as above but substitute the following for the pesto and cilantro. Pour over shrimp, toss until shrimp are coated, and serve.

¾ cup prepared red pepper pesto
2 tablespoons canned diced tomatoes, drained
3 tablespoons toasted pine nuts
¼ teaspoon salt

Stuffed Cherry Tomatoes

Mascarpone is an Italian double-cream cheese made from cow's milk. You can substitute sour cream if you can't find mascarpone.

PREP TIME: 20 MINUTES • MAKES: 96

48 cherry tomatoes (about 1½
  pounds)
1 package (5 ounces) herb-garlic
  cream cheese, softened
½ cup mascarpone cheese, softened

1. Cut each tomato in half. Scoop out and discard the seeds and pulp.

2. In a small bowl, combine the two cheeses and stir until well mixed. Spoon the cheese mixture evenly into the tomato shells.

Prosciutto-Stuffed Mushrooms

Select the smallest mushrooms you can find, for an easy-to-pop-into-your-mouth appetizer.

PREP TIME: 20 MINUTES • **BAKE TIME: 8 TO 10 MINUTES** • **MAKES: 20 TO 24**

1 package (8 ounces) fresh button mushrooms

¼ cup fresh bread crumbs

2 ounces sliced prosciutto ham, finely chopped

2 tablespoons shredded Parmesan cheese

1 tablespoon olive oil

1. Heat oven to 425°F. Rinse and drain mushrooms. Remove stems and discard.

2. In a small bowl, combine bread crumbs, prosciutto, cheese and olive oil until well mixed. Spoon ham mixture evenly into mushroom caps. Arrange on an ungreased baking sheet. Bake 8 to 10 minutes. Serve warm.

VARIATON

Herb-Garlic Stuffed Mushrooms
Prepare mushrooms as above, but omit the cheese, prosciutto, oil, and bread crumbs. Substitute 1 package (5 ounces) herb-garlic cheese. Fill and bake as above.

Prosciutto-Wrapped Figs

Look for dark Mission figs for this appetizer. The contrast of the sweet fruit and the salty ham makes this a perfect starter.

PREP TIME: 15 MINUTES • MAKES: 20 TO 24 SERVINGS

1 package (4 ounces) sliced prosciutto
10 to 12 fresh figs
3½ tablespoons garlic cheese spread

1. Cut each prosciutto slice into quarters. Cut each fig in half; quarter any figs that are extra large.

2. Spoon a ½ teaspoon garlic cheese on the cut side of each fig. Wrap a piece of prosciutto around each fig. Secure with a toothpick. Serve immediately.

Bacon-Stuffed Tomatoes

If you love BLTs, this is the appetizer for you.

PREP TIME: 30 MINUTES • MAKES: 36 TO 48

1 pound fresh cherry tomatoes
10 slices precooked bacon, chopped
2 green onions, finely chopped
¼ cup mayonnaise

1. Cut each tomato in half. Scoop out and discard the seeds and pulp.

2. In a small bowl, combine the bacon, onions, and mayonnaise; stir until well mixed. Spoon the bacon mixture evenly into the tomato shells. (Can be made ahead, covered, and refrigerated up to 2 hours. Bring to room temperature before serving.)

Tortellini Bites

Sprinkle some shredded Parmesan over the tortellini for a lovely presentation. Serve with toothpicks alongside.

PREP TIME: 5 MINUTES • COOK TIME: 5 TO 6 MINUTES • MAKES: 10 SERVINGS

1 package (16 ounces) frozen
  tortellini with cheese
2 tablespoons prepared refrigerated
  basil pesto
1 tablespoon grated lemon zest
2 tablespoons chopped fresh parsley
Shredded Parmesan cheese, for
  garnish (optional)

1. Cook tortellini according to package directions. Drain.

2. In a large bowl, combine pesto, lemon zest, and parsley; stir until well combined. Add the drained tortellini and toss until coated. Serve warm, garnished with shredded Parmesan cheese, if desired.

Marinated Bocconcini

Mini mozzarella balls are perfect for a quick bite. These are better made 24 hours ahead.

PREP TIME: 5 MINUTES • MAKES: ABOUT 16

½ pound fresh mozzarella mini balls
   (bocconcini)
¼ cup olive oil
1 teaspoon hot pepper flakes
1 tablespoon chopped fresh sage
Dash freshly ground pepper

Combine all ingredients in a small bowl. Toss until cheese is well coated. Cover and refrigerate at least 4 hours. (Can be made ahead, covered, and refrigerated up to 2 days.) Bring to room temperature before serving. Serve with toothpicks.

Mexican Meatballs

Look for masa harina, a flour made from dried corn, in the Latin section of the supermarket. The flavor improves if the meatballs are made a day ahead.

PREP TIME: 30 MINUTES • **COOK TIME: 25 MINUTES** • **MAKES: 36**

1 teaspoon chopped garlic

1 teaspoon salt

1 pound ground meatloaf mix
   (a combination of veal, pork,
   and beef)

¼ cup masa harina

1 egg yolk

2 tablespoons chopped fresh cilantro,
   divided

1 jar (16 ounces) chipotle salsa

1. In a large bowl, combine the garlic and salt and, using the back of a wooden spoon, rub to a paste. Add the ground meat, masa harina, egg yolk, and 1 tablespoon cilantro. Mix well.

2. In a large skillet, heat the salsa over medium-high heat to a simmer. Meanwhile, using a small ice-cream scoop, shape ground meat mixture into 1-inch balls.

3. Add meatballs to the simmering salsa; cover, reduce heat to medium, and cook 10 minutes. Turn meatballs. Continue cooking 15 more minutes. (Can be made ahead, cooled, covered, and refrigerated up to 24 hours. Reheat over low heat for 20 minutes.) Serve in a chafing dish or slow cooker with toothpicks. Garnish with the remaining cilantro.

Sweet-and-Sour Meatballs

This classic recipe gets a hint of heat with bottled chipotle sauce.

PREP TIME: 5 MINUTES • COOK TIME: 13 MINUTES PLUS STANDING • MAKES: 24

1 jar (12 ounces) chili sauce
1 jar (12 ounces) grape jelly
½ teaspoon bottled chipotle sauce
1 package (24 ounces) fully cooked
    appetizer-size turkey meatballs

1. In a large saucepan, heat chili sauce, jelly, and chipotle sauce over medium heat 5 minutes, stirring occasionally until jelly melts.

2. Add meatballs and stir until meatballs are coated. Cover; reduce heat to medium and cook 8 minutes, stirring occasionally. Remove from heat and let stand, covered, for 5 minutes.

3. Serve warm in chafing dish or slow cooker. Serve with toothpicks or a fork.

Swedish Meatballs

This updated version of the classic will become your must-have hot appetizer dish.

PREP TIME: 10 MINUTES • COOK TIME: 10 MINUTES • MAKES: 12 SERVINGS

1 envelope onion soup mix
½ cup water
1 package (24 ounces) fully cooked
    appetizer-size turkey meatballs
1 cup sour cream
¼ cup chopped fresh dill

1. In a large saucepan, combine onion soup mix and water; stir until well mixed. Add meatballs and stir until meatballs are coated. Cover and cook over medium heat for 5 minutes.

2. Meanwhile, in a medium bowl, combine sour cream and dill. Pour over meatballs in the saucepan; cover and cook 5 more minutes, stirring occasionally. (Can be made ahead, covered, and refrigerated up to 3 days. Reheat in a saucepan over medium heat for 10 minutes.)

3. Serve warm in a chafing dish or slow cooker. Serve with toothpicks or a fork.

VARIATION

Meatballs Puttanesca
Omit the onion soup mix, water, sour cream and fresh dill. Heat 1½ cups jarred puttanesca sauce. Add meatballs and stir until meatballs are coated. Cook 10 minutes, then add 2 tablespoons chopped fresh basil. Serve as directed above.

Stuffed Dates

Careful! These are addictive.

PREP TIME: 10 MINUTES • MAKES: 20

1 package (3 ounces) cream cheese,
    softened
1 tablespoon heavy cream
20 whole pitted dates
20 whole natural toasted almonds

1. In a small bowl, beat the cream cheese and heavy cream until smooth.

2. Cut dates almost in half. Spoon about 1 teaspoon cream cheese into each date. Top cream cheese with an almond. (Can be made ahead, covered, and refrigerated up to 24 hours. Bring to room temperature before serving.)

Tipsy Pineapple

A serving of a sweet in a sea of salty appetizers is a welcome pleasure.

PREP TIME: 5 MINUTES • MAKES: 8 TO 10 SERVINGS

1 can (20 ounces) chunk pineapple, or
    2 cups cubed fresh pineapple
1 cup vodka
3 whole star anise

Combine all ingredients in a freezerproof container. Cover and freeze up to 1 week. Thaw slightly, remove star anise, and serve with toothpicks.

Wraps, Rolls, and More

Surprise Cheese Puffs

There are a variety of stuffed olives on the market today; feel free to substitute them for the traditional olives—but warn guests about the jalapeño-stuffed ones.

PREP TIME: 30 MINUTES • **BAKE TIME: 15 MINUTES** • **MAKES: 30**

1 cup (4 ounces) shredded Cheddar
   cheese
1 stick (½ cup) butter, softened
1 cup all-purpose flour
½ teaspoon paprika
30 small pimiento-stuffed olives,
   well drained

1. In a large mixer bowl, combine cheese, butter, flour, and paprika. Beat for 1 minute, scraping the sides of the bowl occasionally, until a soft dough forms.

2. Heat oven to 400°F. Drain olives thoroughly on paper towels. Roll a table-spoonful of dough around each olive. (If dough becomes too soft, refrigerate for 30 minutes; then continue rolling.)

3. Arrange dough balls 2 inches apart on an ungreased baking sheet. Bake 15 minutes. Serve warm.

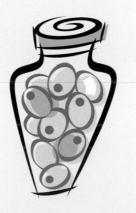

Cornmeal Madeleines

Use silicone mini madeleine pans—they are a dream to use because the baked cornmeal pops out of the pan easily, and the pan cools quickly for baking the remaining batter.

PREP TIME: 10 MINUTES • **BAKE TIME: 8 MINUTES PER BATCH** • **MAKES: 75**

2 mini madeleine pans
1 package (7 ½ ounces) corn bread
   mix
⅛ teaspoon bottled jalapeño sauce
1 cup sour cream or crème fraîche
1 jar (4 ounces) salmon caviar
Fresh dill sprigs or chopped green
   onions, for garnish

1. Heat oven to 400°F. Prepare corn bread mix as package label directs, adding in jalapeño sauce. Spoon by half teaspoons into mini madeleine molds, filling each three-fourths full. Bake 8 minutes. Let stand in pan 4 minutes, then pop out onto a rack to cool completely. Repeat with remaining batter until all batter is used.

2. To serve, top each madeleine with ½ teaspoon each sour cream and caviar. Garnish with dill sprigs or green onions. Serve immediately.

Sausage Rolls

Crescent roll dough is the pastry for this pizza-flavored treat.

PREP TIME: 20 MINUTES PLUS CHILLING • BAKE TIME: 18 MINUTES • MAKES: 40

½ pound sweet Italian sausage
1 package (8 ounces) refrigerated
　　crescent roll dough
8 slices provolone cheese

1. Remove sausage from casings and crumble in a medium skillet. Cook over medium heat 15 minutes, or until it is no longer pink, breaking it up with a wooden spoon as it cooks. Drain well. Let cool thoroughly.

2. Unroll pastry but do not separate into triangles. Pinch the perforations together, making four rectangles. Sprinkle one fourth of the cooked sausage on each dough rectangle,

then top each with two slices of cheese. Roll up from long edge and place each roll, seam-side down, on a sheet of wax paper. Roll up in the paper and refrigerate for 30 minutes.

3. Heat oven to 375°F. Bake the rolls on an ungreased baking sheet for 18 to 20 minutes. To serve, let rolls cool slightly and cut each one into 10 pieces.

VARIATION

Prosciutto and Mozzarella Rolls
Omit sausage and provolone. Substitute 1 package (3 ounces) thinly sliced prosciutto and 8 thin slices mozzarella. Prepare and bake as directed above.

Smoked Salmon Blini

Look for the mini blini in the refrigerated section of the deli or gourmet food market.

PREP TIME: **10 MINUTES** • HEAT TIME: **5 MINUTES** • MAKES: **24**

½ cup chive-and-onion cream cheese, softened
1 tablespoon grated lemon zest
24 mini blini
1 package (8 ounces) sliced smoked salmon
Fresh dill, for garnish

1. In a small bowl, combine the cream cheese and lemon zest; stir until well mixed. Set aside.

2. Heat oven to 425°F. Arrange the blini on an ungreased baking sheet and warm in the oven 5 minutes.

3. Trim the salmon into bite-sized pieces. Spread cream cheese on each blini. Top with salmon. Garnish each with a dill sprig.

Chicken Empanadas

These are great do-ahead party treats. The pastry should be rolled as thin as possible.

PREP TIME: 50 MINUTES • **BAKE TIME: 20 MINUTES PER BATCH** • **MAKES: 32 TO 36**

2 teaspoons olive oil
2 tablespoons minced onion
1 package (6 ounces) roasted chicken breast strips, chopped
½ cup jalapeño cream cheese (half of an 8-ounce tub)
2 tablespoons chopped cilantro
1 package (9 ounces) pie crust mix
1 egg yolk, mixed with 2 teaspoons water

1. In a small skillet, heat the oil. Add the onion and cook until tender, about 2 minutes. Spoon onion into a medium bowl; stir in chicken, cream cheese, and cilantro. Set aside.

2. Prepare pie crust mix according to package directions. Roll out half the pastry to an 11-inch circle. Cut out rounds with a 3-inch biscuit cutter. Place a level teaspoon of filling on one side of each pastry round. Brush edges of pastry rounds with egg mixture and fold over filling. Press edges with the tines of a fork to seal. Arrange pastries 1 inch apart on an ungreased baking sheet. Brush the top of each pastry with egg mixture. Repeat with remaining dough, filling, and egg mixture, rerolling scraps as necessary.

3. Heat oven to 425°F. Bake until golden, about 18 minutes. (Can be made ahead, cooled, and stored in a freezerproof container, and frozen up to 1 month. Reheat in a 350°F oven for 10 minutes.) Serve warm.

Vegetarian Samosas

The fiery filling in these Indian-inspired snacks is cooled with a mint-yogurt dipping sauce.

PREP TIME: 45 MINUTES • **BAKE TIME: 20 MINUTES** • **MAKES: 44 TO 48**

2 packages (9 ounces each) pie crust mix
1 tablespoon olive oil
1 tablespoon butter
½ cup minced onion
1 tablespoon minced fresh ginger
1 ½ teaspoons curry powder
1 cup prepared mashed potatoes
⅓ cup frozen tiny green peas
1 egg yolk, mixed with 1 tablespoon water
2 cups plain yogurt
¼ cup chopped fresh mint
½ teaspoon cumin
Dash salt

1. In a large saucepan, heat oil and butter until butter is melted. Add the onion, ginger and curry powder and cook until onion is tender, about 3 minutes. Stir in potatoes and peas. Cover and cook over medium heat about 4 minutes until heated through; set aside.

2. Heat oven to 400°F. Prepare pie crust mix, one package at a time, according to package directions. Roll out half of the pastry to a 10-inch circle. Cut out rounds with a 2½-inch biscuit cutter. Place a level teaspoon filling on each pastry round. Brush edge of pastry with egg mixture and fold to close. Press edges with the tines of a fork to seal. Arrange pastries 1 inch apart on an ungreased baking sheet. Brush top of pastry with egg mixture. Repeat with remaining dough, filling, and egg mixture, re-rolling scraps. Bake until golden, about 20 minutes. Serve warm.

3. In a small bowl, combine yogurt, mint, cumin and dash salt. Serve with samosas.

Pigs in a Blanket

These are such a nostalgic taste—regardless of how many you make there will not be any left when the party is over.

PREP TIME: 20 MINUTES • BAKE TIME: 10 TO 12 MINUTES PER BATCH • MAKES: 44

2 packages (8 ounces each)
    refrigerated crescent roll dough
2 tablespoons honey mustard, plus
    more for serving
1 package (14 ounces) all-beef
    cocktail franks

1. Heat oven to 375°F. Work with one package of crescent dough at a time. Keep the other refrigerated. Remove the dough from the package, unroll, and cut between the perforations. Then cut each of the 4 large triangles lengthwise into 4 smaller triangles and spread the dough with half the honey mustard.

2. Place a frank at the wide edge of the dough and roll up. Transfer to an ungreased baking sheet with the seam tucked under. Repeat with remaining franks, dough, and honey mustard. (All the dough may not be used.)

3. Bake, 12 per baking sheet, until dough is puffy and light golden, 10 to 12 minutes. Serve warm, with additional honey mustard for dipping.

Asparagus Roll-ups

A classic appetizer that never goes out of style.

PREP TIME: 15 MINUTES • BAKE TIME: 8 TO 10 MINUTES • MAKES: 32

8 slices white sandwich bread, crusts removed
¼ cup chive-and-onion cream cheese
16 frozen asparagus spears, thawed
2 tablespoons butter, melted

1. Heat oven to 425°F. With a rolling pin, flatten each bread slice. Cut each slice in half.

2. Spread cream cheese on each bread slice. Place one asparagus spear on each; roll up. Brush the tops of the bread with melted butter. Arrange, seam-side down, on a lightly buttered baking sheet. Bake until the bread is lightly toasted, 8 to 10 minutes. To serve, cut each roll in half.

VARIATION

Ham and Asparagus Roll-ups
Prepare as above but omit the cream cheese. Add 2 tablespoons Dijon mustard and ¼ pound thinly sliced ham. Spread bread with mustard, then top with ham, cut to fit the bread, and the asparagus. Roll up. Brush with butter and bake as directed above.

White Bean-Parmesan Bruschetta

Use either regular white beans or cannellini for this easy hors d'oeuvre.

PREP TIME: 10 MINUTES • BROIL TIME: 5 MINUTES • MAKES: ABOUT 40

1 loaf (1 pound) French bread
4 tablespoons olive oil
1 can (15 ounces) white beans,
    drained and rinsed
½ cup chopped fresh sage
½ cup freshly grated Parmesan
    cheese

1. Heat broiler. Cut bread in half length-wise and place, cut-side up, on a baking sheet. Brush cut sides with oil.

2. In a small bowl, mash the beans with the back of a fork. Stir in remaining olive oil and sage. Spoon bean mixture evenly over cut sides of bread. Sprinkle with cheese.

3. Broil 3 inches from heat source until cheese begins to soften and edges of the bread brown lightly, about 5 minutes. Cut into 1-inch slices and serve immediately.

White Bean-Prosciutto Bruschetta
Omit fresh sage. Substitute 2 tablespoons chopped fresh basil and add 2 ounces sliced prosciutto, chopped. Prepare as directed above.

Roasted Pepper Bruschetta

A great last-minute entertaining hors d'oeuvre piled onto French bread.

PREP TIME: 10 MINUTES • BROIL TIME: 5 MINUTES • MAKES: ABOUT 40

1 loaf (1 pound) French bread
4 tablespoons olive oil
1 cup crumbled garlic and herb feta
   cheese (from a 6-ounce package)
1 cup roasted red pepper, drained and
   sliced
1 cup chopped cherry tomatoes

1. Heat broiler. Slice the bread in half lengthwise and place, cut-side up, on a broiler pan. Brush cut sides with oil.

2. In a small bowl, combine remaining olive oil, cheese, red pepper, and tomatoes; toss. Spoon pepper mixture evenly over cut sides of bread halves. Sprinkle with cheese.

3. Broil 3 inches from heat source until cheese begins to soften and edges of the bread brown lightly, about 5 minutes. Cut into 1-inch slices and serve immediately.

Gorgonzola and Caramelized Onion Crostini

The key is the long, slow cooking of the onions.

PREP TIME: 40 MINUTES • **BAKE TIME: 13 MINUTES** • **MAKES: 32**

2 tablespoons olive oil
3 medium onions, thinly sliced
1½ teaspoons balsamic vinegar
4 ounces cream cheese, softened
1/3 cup crumbled Gorgonzola cheese
32 (½-inch-thick) slices French bread

1. In a large skillet, heat the olive oil for 1 minute over high heat. Add the onions and reduce heat to medium; cook, stirring occasionally, 30 minutes. Stir in the vinegar.

2. In a small bowl, stir the cream and Gorgonzola cheeses until well mixed.

3. Heat oven to 425°F. Arrange bread slices on a baking sheet. Toast bread for 5 minutes to crisp. Spread tops of the bread slices with cheese mixture, then top with onions. Return to oven and bake until cheese is melted and bubbly, about another 8 minutes. Serve warm.

VARIATION

Gorgonzola-Caramelized Onion Crostini with Fig Jam
Prepare as above through step 2. Then as the bread is pulled from the oven, spoon ⅓ cup fig jam evenly onto the baked cheese-topped bread. Return to oven and bake as above.

Dill Shrimp Crostini

If you can't find fresh dill, then use dried.

PREP TIME: 20 MINUTES • **BAKE TIME: 8 MINUTES** • **MAKES: 36**

36 slices party rye bread

¼ cup honey mustard

1 package (8 ounces) sliced dill
    Havarti cheese

36 medium shelled and deveined
    shrimp, thawed if frozen and tails
    removed

2 tablespoons chopped fresh chives or
    green onions

1 tablespoon chopped fresh dill

1. Heat oven to 400°F. Place bread on a baking sheet. Bake for 5 minutes to crisp.

2. Spread one side of each bread slice with honey mustard. Cut the cheese slices into 2-inch squares and place on bread. Top each with 1 shrimp. Sprinkle with chives and dill. Bake on bottom rack of oven for 5 minutes. Serve warm.

Parmesan Toasts

Served plain, these tasty toasts make a great addition to your party table. But they also are great with a bowl of soup!

PREP TIME: 15 MINUTES • BAKE TIME: 10 MINUTES • MAKES: 24

1 loaf Italian bread, cut into 24
   (¼-inch) slices
¼ cup olive oil
1 cup grated Parmesan cheese

1. Heat oven to 400°F. Line a baking sheet with foil. Arrange bread slices on prepared baking sheet and brush tops with olive oil. Sprinkle cheese generously on each bread slice.

2. Bake until edges of bread and cheese are golden, about 10 minutes. (Can be made ahead, covered, and stored in an airtight container up to 1 week.)

Mini Roast-Beef Sandwiches

The horseradish cream can be made ahead–in fact, it's better if it is.

PREP TIME: **20 MINUTES** • **MAKES: 48**

1 cup sour cream
½ cup mayonnaise
2 tablespoons prepared horseradish
1½ teaspoons Dijon mustard
1 package of 24 party rolls,
    cut in half horizontally
1 pound rare roast beef or tenderloin,
    thinly sliced
Chopped parsley, for garnish

1. In a small bowl, combine sour cream, mayonnaise, horseradish, and mustard; stir until well mixed. (Can be made ahead, covered, and refrigerated up to 24 hours.)

2. Spread the cut sides of each roll with horseradish cream. Top with a slice of beef and then add another dollop of horseradish cream. Just before serving, garnish with chopped parsley.

Roast Turkey-Brie Sandwiches

If you can't find ciabatta, substitute plain foccacia. These sandwiches must be made ahead.

PREP TIME: 15 MINUTES • **CHILL TIME: 4 HOURS** • **MAKES: 20**

1 loaf ciabatta bread or foccacia
⅓ cup mayonnaise
2 tablespoons prepared basil pesto
14 ounces Brie cheese
¼ cup cranberry sauce
½ pound sliced roast turkey

1. Slice the ciabatta loaf in half lengthwise. In a small bowl, mix together the mayonnaise and pesto. Thinly slice the Brie. To keep the knife blade from sticking to the cheese, run the blade under hot water and dry it off after every few slices.

2. Spread the mayonnaise mixture on both cut sides of the bread. On the bottom, evenly layer Brie, cranberry sauce, and turkey; add top bread slice. Wrap in plastic wrap. Place between two baking sheets and weigh down the top one with two heavy cans. Refrigerate up to 4 hours.

3. To serve, unwrap and cut each sandwich into 2-inch squares or triangles.

Italian Toasted Cheese Sandwiches

Semolina bread, made from the flour used to make pasta, can be found in your local bakery. If you can't find it, you can substitute thinly sliced Italian bread.

PREP TIME: 15 MINUTES • **COOK TIME: 10 MINUTES PER BATCH** • **MAKES: 18**

12 slices thinly sliced semolina bread
½ stick (¼ cup) butter, softened
1 tablespoon anchovy paste
¼ pound sliced prosciutto
¼ pound sliced mozzarella cheese

1. Trim the crusts from the bread; discard the crusts. Spread butter evenly on one side of each bread slice.

2. Place half the bread, butter-side down, on a sheet of wax paper. Spread anchovy paste on the bread and add the prosciutto and cheese. Top with remaining bread slices, butter-side up.

3. Heat a large skillet over medium-high heat. Grill the sandwiches in batches until toasted, 4 or 5 minutes per side.

4. To serve, cut each sandwich into 5 or 6 lengthwise pieces. Wrap each piece in a paper cocktail napkin.

Croque Monsieur

Your guests will appreciate the napkins wrapped around these buttery little sandwiches.

PREP TIME: 15 MINUTES • COOK TIME: 10 MINUTES PER BATCH • MAKES: 18

12 slices thinly sliced white bread
½ stick (¼ cup) butter, softened
1 tablespoon honey mustard
¼ pound sliced Black Forest ham or
    other good-quality ham
¼ pound sliced Gruyère cheese

1. Trim the crusts from the bread; discard the crusts. Spread butter evenly on one side of each bread slice.

2. Place half the bread, butter-side down, on a sheet of wax paper. Spread the mustard on the bread and add the ham and cheese. Top with remaining bread slices, butter-side up.

3. Heat a large skillet over medium-high heat. Grill the sandwiches in batches 4 or 5 minutes per side until toasted.

4. To serve, cut each sandwich into 3 lengthwise pieces. Wrap each piece in a paper cocktail napkin.

Roast Pork with Lime Mayonnaise

Pork tenderloin is an ideal party food–sliced, it's a perfect fit for a baguette round.

PREP TIME: 15 MINUTES • ROAST TIME: 20 TO 25 MINUTES • MAKES: 36 PIECES

1 pound boneless marinated pepper
   and garlic pork tenderloin
2 teaspoons chili powder
1 teaspoon kosher salt
½ cup mayonnaise
½ teaspoon lime zest
1 tablespoon lime juice
1 baguette, thinly sliced

1. Heat oven to 425°F. Remove meat from wrappings; discard the marinade. Pat meat dry with paper towels. Rub the chili powder and salt on the meat. Place meat in a roasting pan and roast for 20 to 25 minutes until a meat thermometer inserted into the thickest part of the meat reads 155°F. Cool to room temperature. Slice meat into ¼-inch-thick rounds.

2. In a small bowl, combine the mayonnaise, lime zest, and juice; stir. Spread a small amount of the mixture on each bread slice. Top each with a pork slice and a dab of lime mayonnaise.

VARIATION

Pork with Apple Chutney and Blue Cheese Omit chili powder and lime mayonnaise. Substitute ½ cup prepared apple chutney and ½ cup crumbled blue cheese. To serve, spread each bread slice with chutney and top with pork slice and a dab of chutney. Sprinkle with blue cheese.

Ham and Dijon Mini Biscuits

These are perfect for a brunch buffet.

PREP TIME: 20 MINUTES • **BAKE TIME: 10 TO 12 MINUTES** • **MAKES: ABOUT 27**

2¼ cups all-purpose baking mix
⅔ cup milk
2 tablespoons butter, melted
2 tablespoons Dijon mustard
¾ pound sliced deli ham

1. Heat oven to 450°F. In a medium bowl, combine baking mix and milk; stir until a dough forms.

2. Remove dough from bowl and place on a lightly floured surface. Knead dough about 10 times, then roll out to ⅓ inch thick. Cut out biscuits using a 1½-inch round cookie cutter. Place biscuits on ungreased cookie sheet. Bake 10 to 12 minutes.

3. Brush the tops of the biscuits with melted butter. Split and spread bottoms with mustard. Top each with sliced ham and then with the top halves of biscuits.

VARIATION

Ham Biscuits with White Truffle Honey
Prepare and bake biscuits as above but omit the mustard. Increase the melted butter by 2 tablespoons (for a total of 4 tablespoons) and brush cut sides with butter. Spread bottom sides evenly with ¼ cup white truffle honey; top with ham and then with top halves of biscuits.

Mini Grilled Reubens

This sandwich gained national appeal when it won a sandwich contest in 1956.

PREP TIME: 15 MINUTES • COOK TIME: 4 MINUTES PER BATCH • MAKES: 32

⅔ cup butter, softened

32 slices cocktail rye bread (from a
    12-ounce loaf)

⅔ cup Russian dressing

4 ounces sliced deli corned beef

6 tablespoons well-drained sauerkraut

4 ounces sliced Swiss cheese

1. Spread butter evenly on one side of each bread slice. Place the bread, butter-side down, on wax paper. Spread 1 teaspoon Russian dressing on each bread slice. Top half the bread slices with corned beef, folding the meat to fit on the bread. Spoon 1 teaspoon sauerkraut on top of each of the corned beef slices. Top each with Swiss cheese, folding cheese to fit the bread slices. Cover with remaining bread, butter-side up. (Can be assembled ahead, covered, and refrigerated until ready to grill.)

2. Heat a large skillet over medium-high heat or heat sandwich grill. Add half of the sandwiches and cook 2 minutes per side. Serve immediately. The sandwiches can be cut in half, if desired.

Pissaladière

This classic appetizer is a specialty dish of Nice, France.

PREP TIME: 40 MINUTES PLUS RISING • BAKE TIME: 15 MINUTES • MAKES: 36 PIECES

1 package (16 ounces) hot roll mix
6 tablespoons olive oil, divided
4 medium onions, thinly sliced
¼ teaspoon thyme
Salt and pepper to taste
2 garlic cloves, minced
2 cans (2 ounces each) flat anchovy
    fillets, packed in oil and drained
½ cup shredded Parmesan cheese
½ cup Niçoise olives, pitted

1. Prepare the hot roll mix as directed on the package for pizza recipe using olive oil. Place in a warm spot to rise.

2. Heat 4 tablespoons oil in a large skillet over high heat. Add the onions and cook until onions become transparent, stirring frequently. Reduce the heat to medium-low. Cover and cook for 30 minutes until very tender, stirring occasionally. Remove from heat and stir in the thyme, salt, and pepper; cool. In a mini food processor, combine the garlic, 6 anchovies, and 2 tablespoons oil; pulse to form a paste. Cut remaining anchovies into strips.

3. Heat oven to 450°F. Grease a baking sheet. Punch down dough and roll out to a 12-inch square on a lightly floured surface; transfer to baking sheet. Spread anchovy mixture evenly over the dough. Sprinkle on half the cheese. Layer on onions, anchovy strips, olives, and remaining cheese. Bake until crust is golden, 15 minutes. Let cool to room temperature and cut into 2-inch squares.

Greek Tomato Pizza

Be sure to wrap any unused phyllo well to prevent it from drying out.

PREP TIME: 25 MINUTES • **BAKE TIME: 15 MINUTES** • **MAKES: 25 PIECES**

8 sheets phyllo dough
⅓ cup butter, melted
3 tablespoons plain dried bread
   crumbs
1 package (6 ounces) shredded
   mozzarella cheese (1½ cups)
2 medium fresh tomatoes, thinly sliced
1½ teaspoons oregano
¼ teaspoon kosher salt

1. Heat oven to 450°F. Brush the bottom of a 15½ x 10½ x 1-inch jelly roll pan with butter. Place one sheet of phyllo dough in prepared pan; cover remaining phyllo with plastic wrap. Brush with butter and sprinkle lightly with bread crumbs. Repeat layering phyllo dough, brushing each layer with butter, and sprinkling each layer except the top with bread crumbs.

2. Spread the cheese evenly on top sheet of phyllo, arrange tomatoes over the cheese, and sprinkle with oregano and salt. Bake 15 minutes. Cool slightly, then cut into pieces.

Asparagus Pizza

These classic French flavors combine for a new twist on pizza.

PREP TIME: 25 MINUTES • BAKE TIME: 15 MINUTES • MAKES: 25 PIECES

8 sheets phyllo dough
⅓ cup butter, melted
3 tablespoons plain dried bread
    crumbs
1 package (6 ounces) shredded swiss
    cheese (1½ cups)
¾ pound frozen asparagus, thawed
    and cut into 1-inch pieces
1½ teaspoons chopped tarragon
¼ teaspoon kosher salt

1. Heat oven to 450°F. Brush the bottom of a 15½ x 10½ x 1-inch jelly roll pan with butter. Place one sheet of phyllo dough in prepared pan; cover remaining phyllo with plastic wrap. Brush with butter and sprinkle lightly with bread crumbs. Repeat layering phyllo dough, brushing each layer with butter, and sprinkling each layer except the top with bread crumbs.

2. Spread the cheese evenly on top sheet of phyllo, arrange asparagus over the cheese, and sprinkle with tarragon and salt. Bake 15 minutes. Cool slightly, then cut into pieces.

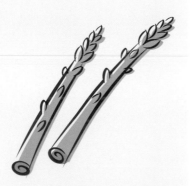

Tomato-Onion Foccacia

Serve this instead of garlic bread at your next dinner party!

PREP TIME: 30 MINUTES PLUS RISING • BAKE TIME: 20 MINUTES • MAKES: 48 PIECES

1 package (16 ounces) hot roll mix
Olive oil
2 teaspoons minced dried rosemary
    or basil
1 teaspoon kosher salt
1 medium onion, thinly sliced
24 cherry tomatoes, halved

1. Heat oven to 425°F. Prepare hot roll mix and knead as package label directs for pizza recipe using olive oil. Place in a warm place to rise.

2. Grease a 15½ x 10½ x 1-inch jelly roll pan with 1 tablespoon olive oil. After rising, punch dough down; roll dough into 15 x 10-inch rectangle and transfer to prepared pan. Let dough rest 10 minutes. Stretch dough again to fit into the pan.

3. Spread 3 tablespoons olive oil on dough. Sprinkle with rosemary and salt. Arrange the onions and tomatoes, cut-side up, evenly over the dough. Bake 20 minutes. Remove to a cutting board and cut into 48 pieces. Serve warm.

Puff Pastry Tomato Pizza

Puff pastry makes a very light crust and a great change from the usual pizza crust. Poking the crust with a fork prevents the pastry from puffing.

PREP TIME: 15 MINUTES • BAKE TIME: 20 MINUTES • MAKES: 24

1 sheet frozen puff pastry (from a 17.3-ounce package), thawed

1 package (5.2 ounces) garlic cheese, at room temperature

¼ cup sour cream

¼ teaspoon dried basil

12 to 14 cherry tomatoes, halved

1. Heat oven to 425°F. Unfold the sheet of puff pastry. Roll to a 14-inch square. Transfer to a baking sheet. Pierce the pastry all over with a fork.

2. In a small bowl, combine the garlic cheese and sour cream and stir until smooth. Spread cheese mixture evenly over the pastry. Sprinkle evenly with the basil. Place tomatoes, cut-side down, on the cheese. Bake until crust is lightly browned, 20 minutes. Transfer to cutting board and cut into 24 pieces. Serve warm.

Mushroom Phyllo Tarts

The food processor makes short work of finely chopping the mushrooms.

PREP TIME: 35 MINUTES • BAKE TIME: 15 TO 18 MINUTES • MAKES: 45

2 tablespoons butter
¼ cup chopped shallots
2 packages (8 ounces each) sliced
   fresh mushrooms
1 teaspoon salt
1 container (8 ounces) chive and onion
   cream cheese
3 packages (2.1 ounces each) mini
   phyllo dough shells

1. Preheat oven to 400°F. Line a baking sheet with parchment paper. Arrange dough shells on baking sheet; set aside.

2. In a large skillet, melt butter. Add the shallots and cook 1 minute. Add the mushrooms and salt and cook until all liquid has evaporated, 6 to 8 minutes. Cool slightly.

3. Transfer the mushroom mixture to the bowl of a food processor with the steel blade attached. Pulse until finely chopped. Add the cream cheese and pulse until smooth.

4. Spoon filling evenly into dough shells. Bake until golden, about 10 minutes.

VARIATION

Mushroom Phyllo Rolls
Increase the butter to 6 tablespoons. Follow rolling and baking directions for **Spinach Phyllo Rolls**, page 126.

Spinach Phyllo Rolls

This Greek-inspired appetizer is freezer-friendly—a boon for party planning.

PREP TIME: 30 MINUTES • **BAKE TIME: 15 TO 18 MINUTES** • **MAKES: 24**

1 package (12 ounces) frozen spinach
    soufflé, thawed
1 package (4 ounces) crumbled feta
    cheese
1 teaspoon dill weed
6 sheets phyllo dough
½ stick (¼ cup) butter, melted
2 tablespoons plain dry bread crumbs

1. Heat oven to 400°F. Grease a large baking sheet. In a medium bowl, combine spinach soufflé, cheese, and dill; stir until well mixed.

2. Place one sheet of phyllo on a sheet of wax paper or a clean towel. (Keep remaining phyllo covered with a damp towel.) Brush lightly with melted butter and sprinkle with 1 tablespoon bread crumbs. Repeat layering with 2 more sheets of phyllo, omitting the bread crumbs. Spread half of the spinach mixture along one long edge of phyllo.

3. Using wax paper as a guide, roll phyllo from long edge jelly-roll fashion. Place, seam-side down, on prepared baking pan. Press ends to seal. With a knife, cut slices about halfway through phyllo at 1-inch intervals. Repeat with remaining ingredients, making one more roll.

4. Bake rolls until golden brown, 15 to 18 minutes. Let cool slightly and cut rolls all the way through. Serve warm. (Can be made ahead, stored in a freezerproof container, and frozen up to 1 month. Reheat in a 400°F oven for 8 minutes.)

Fruited Baked Brie

An elegant (and easy!) addition to any buffet table.

PREP TIME: 20 MINUTES • BAKE TIME: 30 MINUTES • MAKES: 16 SERVINGS

1 package (17.3 ounces) frozen puff
    pastry, thawed (2 sheets)
1 wheel (2.2 pounds) Brie cheese,
    about 8 inches in diameter
⅓ cup dried cranberries
⅓ cup sliced almonds, toasted
¼ cup orange marmalade
1 egg yolk, mixed with 1 tablespoon
    water
Assorted crackers, for serving

1. Heat oven to 400°F. Line a baking
sheet with parchment paper; set aside.
Roll one piece of pastry on a lightly
floured surface into a 12-inch square.
Cut a 1-inch strip from pastry; set aside.
Using a 9-inch round cake pan as a
guide, trim the square to a 9-inch circle.
Place the circle on the parchment-lined
baking sheet. Repeat the rolling and cutting
with a second piece of pastry. Set aside.

2. Center Brie on the pastry on the baking
sheet. In a small bowl, combine the cranberries, almonds, and marmalade; stir.
Spread mixture on top of Brie. Gently fold
the pastry up the side of the cheese. (It will
not come all the way up.) Carefully place
the other pastry circle on top of Brie; fold
edges down. The edges may not meet.

3. Brush pastry with egg mixture. Wrap
reserved strips of pastry around outside
edge of brie to seal pastry rounds. Brush
with egg mixture. (Can be made ahead,
covered, and refrigerated up to 24 hours.)
Bake until pastry is golden, about 30
minutes. Let stand 20 minutes at room
temperature before serving.

Onion-Walnut Baked Brie

This unusual flavor combination is perfect for an elegant wine-and-cheese party.

PREP TIME: 20 MINUTES • BAKE TIME: 30 MINUTES • MAKES: 16 SERVINGS

1 package (17.3 ounces) frozen puff
    pastry, thawed (2 sheets)
1 wheel (2.2 pounds) Brie cheese,
    about 8 inches in diameter
1/3 cup garlic and onion jam
1/3 cup sugared walnuts, chopped
1 egg yolk, mixed with 1 tablespoon
    water
Assorted crackers, for serving

1. Heat oven to 400°F. Line a baking sheet with parchment paper; set aside. Roll one piece of pastry on a lightly floured surface into a 12-inch square. Cut a 1-inch strip from pastry; set aside. Using a 9-inch round cake pan as a guide, trim the square to a 9-inch circle. Place the circle on the parchment-lined baking sheet. Repeat the rolling and cutting with a second piece of pastry. Set aside.

2. Center the Brie on the pastry on the baking sheet. In a small bowl, combine the jam and walnuts; stir. Spread mixture on top of Brie. Gently fold the pastry up the side of the cheese. (It will not come all the way up.) Carefully place the other pastry circle on top of Brie; fold edges down. The edges may not meet.

3. Brush pastry with egg mixture. Wrap reserved strips of pastry around outside edge of Brie to seal pastry rounds. Brush with egg mixture. (Can be made ahead, covered, and refrigerated up to 24 hours.) Bake until pastry is golden, about 30 minutes. Let stand 20 minutes at room temperature before serving.

Elegant Starters

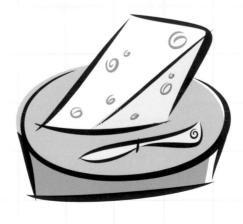

Moroccan Carrots

Seasoned with cumin and mint, these are a pleasant surprise on a crudité platter.

PREP TIME: 10 MINUTES • COOK TIME: 12 TO 15 MINUTES • MAKES: 8 SERVINGS

2 tablespoons water
2 tablespoons olive oil
2 tablespoons honey
½ teaspoon salt
1½ teaspoons cumin
1 package (16 ounces) baby carrots
¼ cup chopped fresh mint
1 tablespoon fresh lemon juice

1. In a medium saucepan over low heat, combine water, oil, honey, salt, and cumin. Heat until honey is melted.

2. Add carrots and cook over medium-high heat, stirring occasionally, until carrots are tender and most of the liquid has evaporated, about 5 minutes. Cool. To serve, add mint and lemon juice; toss. Serve with toothpicks.

Artichokes with Lemon Cream

Be sure to have a place for guests to deposit the discarded leaves.

PREP TIME: 20 MINUTES • COOK TIME: 40 MINUTES • MAKES: 48 PIECES

4 medium fresh artichokes, stem cut
　off and thorny tips trimmed
1 cup plain yogurt
1 teaspoon grated lemon zest
1 teaspoon lemon juice
3 tablespoons olive oil
¼ teaspoon salt
2 tablespoons chopped fresh mint

1. In a large saucepot over high heat, bring 1 inch of water to boiling. Place the artichokes base-side down in the water; reduce heat to medium, cover, and cook until a fork can be easily inserted into the base, 35 to 40 minutes. Cool. When cool enough to handle, remove the fuzzy choke with a spoon; discard.

2. In a medium bowl, combine the yogurt, lemon zest and juice, olive oil, salt, and mint. Stir well to combine. (Can be made ahead. Cover and refrigerate up to 2 days. Makes about 1½ cups.)

3. To serve, arrange artichokes on a platter and spoon the lemon cream into an adjacent bowl.

Portabello Mushroom Bites

These can be made up to 6 hours ahead and reheated in the oven, perfect for a host who wants to visit with guests.

PREP TIME: 20 MINUTES • MAKES: 24

1 package (10 ounces) all-purpose
    batter fry mix
2 packages (6 ounces each) sliced
    fresh portabello mushrooms
2 cups vegetable oil
Salt
Prepared tartar sauce, for serving

1. Prepare wet and dry batters as directed on the package directions. Dip mushroom slices into the wet batter, then dry batter. Set aside on wax paper.

2. In a large skillet, heat the oil to 365°F on deep-fat thermometer (about 5 minutes over low heat). Add half of the mushrooms and cook, turning once, until golden, about 4 minutes. Drain on paper towels. Repeat with remaining mushrooms. (Can be made ahead, covered, and refrigerated up to 6 hours. Reheat in a 350°F oven for 8 minutes.) Sprinkle with salt.

3. To serve, arrange on a platter with a bowl of tartar sauce for dipping.

Corn Fritters

These silver dollar-sized fritters are just perfect to pop in your mouth. Be careful—they might disappear as quickly as corn chips.

PREP TIME: 10 MINUTES • **COOK TIME: 5 MINUTES PER BATCH** • **MAKES: 32 TO 34**

1 can (16 ounces) whole kernel corn,
    drained
2 large eggs
6 tablespoons baking mix
⅛ teaspoon nutmeg
2 tablespoons vegetable oil
2 tablespoons butter
½ cup sour cream
1 jar (4.2 ounces) sun-dried tomato
    pesto

1. Purée the corn in a food processor with the steel blade attached. In a medium bowl, beat the eggs. Add the puréed corn, baking mix, and nutmeg; stir to combine.

2. In a large skillet, heat the oil and butter until the butter melts. Drop batter by teaspoonfuls onto the hot skillet and cook, turning once, until lightly browned, about 5 minutes. Continue cooking until all batter is used. (Can be made ahead, covered, and refrigerated up to 24 hours. Reheat in a 350°F oven about 5 minutes.)

3. To serve, top fritters with a teaspoon of sour cream and ¼ teaspoon sun-dried tomato pesto.

Zucchini Fritters

These little fritters are great alone, or plunged into one of the dips from Chapter 1 (Romesco Sauce, page 12, is perfect).

PREP TIME: 20 MINUTES • COOK TIME: 6 MINUTES PER BATCH • MAKES: 36

½ pound zucchini, about 2 small

1 large egg

½ cup shredded Mexican-style four-cheese blend (Cheddar, Monterey Jack, queso blanco, and asadero)

2 tablespoons minced onion

⅔ cup all-purpose baking mix

1 teaspoon cumin

2 tablespoons vegetable oil

2 tablespoons butter

½ cup mayonnaise

¼ cup sour cream

¼ cup chopped fresh cilantro

¼ teaspoon hot salt

1. Using a cheese grater, shred zucchini; drain on paper towels. In a large bowl, beat the egg; add cheese and onion. Fold in the zucchini. Stir in baking mix and cumin.

2. Heat a large skillet over medium-high heat or griddle to 365°F. Add vegetable oil and butter and heat until butter melts. Drop batter by teaspoonfuls, 8 at a time. Cook until golden, 2 or 3 minutes, turning once. Repeat with remaining batter. (Can be made ahead, covered, and refrigerated up to 24 hours. Reheat in a 350°F oven for 10 minutes.)

3. In a small bowl, combine mayonnaise, sour cream, cilantro, and hot salt; stir until smooth. Serve fritters warm topped with a dab of sauce.

Sausage Wonton Stars

This spicy appetizer is perfect for a large holiday party. Use two mini-muffin pans for speedier baking.

PREP TIME: 45 MINUTES • BAKE TIME: 10 MINUTES PER BATCH • MAKES:80

1 pound bulk pork sausage

2 cups shredded Cheddar cheese

1 package (8 ounces) cream cheese, softened

1 cup sour cream

1 can (6 ounces) pitted black ripe olives, drained and slice

1 envelope (1.1 ounce) ranch salad dressing and dip mix

1 package (16 ounces) egg roll wrappers, cut into quarters

1. In a large skillet, cook sausage according to package directions. Drain and crumble. Place in a large bowl. Add Cheddar, cream cheese, sour cream, olives, and dressing mix; stir until well combined.

2. Heat the oven to 400°F. Press the egg roll wrapper quarters into the bottom and up the sides of nonstick mini-muffin pan cups. Keep remaining wrappers covered with a damp paper towel to prevent them from drying out.

3. Spoon a tablespoon of the sausage mixture into each wrapper. Bake until filling is bubbly, about 10 minutes. Continue shaping and baking with remaining filling and wrappers. (Can be made ahead, covered and refrigerated up to 2 days. Reheat in a 350°F oven for 5 minutes.) Serve warm.

Sausage in Wine Sauce

Experiment with different flavors of sausage for a twist on this hearty classic.

PREP TIME: 10 MINUTES • **COOK TIME: 10 TO 12 MINUTES** • **MAKES: 32**

1 package (13 ounces) fully cooked
  chicken and apple sausages
1 cup white wine
1 tablespoon brown sugar
2 tablespoons Dijon mustard
2 tablespoons Calvados or apple
  brandy
2 tablespoons chopped fresh parsley

1. Cut each sausage into 8 pieces. Place in a large skillet and pour the wine over. Cook over medium-high heat, until most of the wine has evaporated.

2. Meanwhile, combine brown sugar, mustard, and Calvados; stir until sugar is dissolved. Pour over the sausages and cook 1 minute. Transfer to a serving plate and sprinkle with the parsley. Serve warm with toothpicks.

VARIATION

Traditional Sausage in Wine Sauce
Substitute kielbasa, cut into bite-sized pieces, for the chicken sausage.

Sausage-Stuffed Portabello Mushrooms

This works as a first course, too—leave the mushrooms whole and serve one per guest.

PREP TIME: 20 MINUTES • BAKE TIME: 20 MINUTES • MAKES: 40

10 large (4 inches) portabello
 mushrooms
1 tube (12 ounces) bulk pork sausage
1 cup freshly grated Parmesan cheese
¼ cup chopped fresh parsley
2 garlic cloves, minced
½ teaspoon hot salt

1. Heat the oven to 375°F. Remove stems from mushrooms and reserve. Wipe the tops of the mushrooms with a damp paper towel. Rinse the stems well and drain.

2. Crumble sausage into a medium skillet and cook over medium heat until it is no longer pink, breaking it up with a wooden spoon as it cooks. Drain well.

3. Finely chop mushroom stems. In a large bowl, combine the sausage, chopped mushroom stems, cheese, parsley, garlic and salt; mix well.

4. Lightly oil a baking sheet. Arrange mushroom caps, top-side down, on baking sheet. Spoon ¼ cup filling onto each cap. Bake 15 to 20 minutes. To serve, cut each mushroom into quarters and serve warm.

Santa Fe Terrine

Serve this classic crowd-pleaser at any event—there won't be a morsel left.

PREP TIME: 20 MINUTES • MAKES: 12 SERVINGS

1 can (16 ounces) refried beans
1 envelope (1 ounce) taco seasoning mix
¼ teaspoon bottled hot pepper sauce
1 medium onion, chopped
¾ cup sour cream
1 can (2 ounces) sliced black olives, drained
1 package (8 ounces) shredded Mexican-blend cheese (Monterey Jack and Cheddar)
3 plum tomatoes, chopped
1 ripe avocado, peeled and chopped
3 tablespoons chopped fresh cilantro

1. Spray an 8-inch springform pan with nonstick cooking spray. In a medium bowl, combine refried beans, seasoning mix, and hot pepper sauce. Stir until well combined. Spread bean mixture into the bottom of the prepared pan. Rinse the onion under hot water; drain well.

2. Spread the drained onions over the bean mixture. Layer the sour cream, olives, cheese, and tomatoes over the beans. (Can be made ahead, covered, and refrigerated up to 24 hours.)

3. Just before serving, toss avocado with cilantro and spoon on top of tomatoes. Place pan on a serving plate and remove sides. Serve with tortilla chips.

VARIATION

Santa Fe Beef-and-Bean Terrine
Layer 1 pound cooked, well-drained ground beef on top of the beans. Continue layering as directedabove.

Caviar Terrine

The terrine is best made ahead and the caviar added just before serving, as the black caviar tends to bleed if it sits too long.

PREP TIME: 20 MINUTES • MAKES: 16 SERVINGS

1 pound good-quality egg salad
    (from the deli section)
1 teaspoon fresh lime juice
1 container (16 ounces) prepared
    guacamole
1 cup sour cream
2 tablespoons minced shallots
1 envelope unflavored gelatin
¼ cup water
1 jar (2 ounces) black lumpfish caviar

1. In a 9-inch glass or ceramic pie plate, spread an even layer of egg salad. Stir lime juice into the guacamole; spread it evenly over the egg salad. Cover surface directly with plastic wrap until sour cream-shallot layer is prepared.

2. In a small bowl, combine the sour cream and shallots; set aside. In a microwaveproof cup, sprinkle the gelatin over the water. Microwave on low heat in 15-second intervals, stirring until gelatin is completely dissolved. Cool.

3. Stir 1½ tablespoons liquid gelatin into the sour cream mixture, stirring quickly to mix well. (If the sour cream is too cold and the gelatin too hot, when stirred together, the gelatin will lump in the sour cream.) Discard remaining gelatin. Spread mixture over guacamole layer. Cover with plastic wrap and refrigerate up to 24 hours.

4. Just before serving, spread caviar evenly on top of sour cream. Serve with an assortment of crackers.

Baked Boursin with Tomato

Combining a dried herb (here it is oregano) with readily available fresh parsley enhances the flavor of the dried herb.

PREP TIME: 15 MINUTES • BAKE TIME: 15 MINUTES • MAKES: 8 TO 10 SERVINGS

1 pint cherry tomatoes, quartered

¼ cup grated Parmesan cheese

3 tablespoons chopped fresh parsley, divided

1½ teaspoons oregano, divided

1 package (5.2 ounces) garlic and herb cheese

1 package (5.2 ounces) pepper and herb cheese

½ cup milk

1. Heat oven to 350°F. In a shallow 2-quart baking dish, spread tomatoes in a single layer. In a small bowl, combine Parmesan cheese, 2 tablespoons parsley, and 1 teaspoon oregano. Sprinkle over the tomatoes.

2. In a medium bowl, combine the two herb cheeses and milk. Stir gently until combined but still lumpy. Pour over tomatoes. Sprinkle with remaining parsley and oregano. (Can be made ahead. Cover and refrigerate up to 24 hours. Remove plastic wrap.) Bake until bubbly at the edges, 15 to 18 minutes. Serve with hearty bread or crackers.

Baked Ricotta with Lemon Oil and Sage

Don't be intimidated by the long prep time—your active time is only about an hour.

PREP TIME: 24 HOURS • **BAKE TIME: 60 MINUTES** • **MAKES: 16 SERVINGS**

1 large container (32 ounces)
    whole-milk ricotta cheese
½ cup lemon-flavored olive oil
½ cup fresh sage leaves
¼ teaspoon kosher salt

1. Line a large sieve with two coffee filters or a double layer of cheesecloth, and place over a bowl. Spoon in the ricotta. Cover and refrigerate overnight, allowing it to drain.

2. Heat oven to 400°F. Discard drained liquid in the bowl. Using the paper filter or cheesecloth, lift cheese and transfer to a lightly greased 1½-quart ovenproof bowl.

3. Bake 1 hour or until top is browned. Cool 10 minutes. Lift cheese and filter from bowl and drain again in the sieve for 30 minutes. (Can be made ahead, covered, and refrigerated up to 2 days.)

4. To serve, peel off the paper filter or remove cheesecloth and place the cheese on a platter. In a small skillet, heat the oil. Add sage leaves and cook until aromatic, about 3 minutes. Pour over the cheese. Sprinkle with salt. Serve with crackers.

Baked Ricotta with Red Pepper Pesto

This dish is a perfect way to kick off an Italian-themed dinner party.

PREP TIME: 24 HOURS • BAKE TIME: 60 MINUTES • MAKES: 16 SERVINGS

1 large container (32 ounces) whole-milk ricotta cheese
½ jar (6 ounces) red pepper pesto
½ cup red pepper jelly
¼ teaspoon kosher salt

1. Line a large sieve with two coffee filters or a double layer of cheese cloth, and place over a bowl. Spoon in the ricotta. Cover and refrigerate overnight, allowing it to drain.

2. Heat oven to 400°F. Discard drained liquid in the bowl. Using the paper filter or cheesecloth, lift cheese and transfer to a lightly greased 1½-quart bowl. Bake until the top is browned, about 1 hour. Cool 10 minutes. Lift cheese and filter from bowl and drain again in the sieve for 30 minutes. (Can be made ahead, covered, and refrigerated up to 2 days.)

3. To serve, peel off the paper filter or remove cheesecloth and place the cheese on a platter. In a small saucepan over low heat, warm jelly until melted. Stir in pesto and cook until warmed through, about 3 minutes. Spread over the baked cheese. Sprinkle with salt. Serve with crackers.

Italian Cheese Torta

Serve with toasted Italian bread slices or a firm cracker such as lavasch.

PREP TIME: 30 MINUTES • MAKES: 16 SERVINGS

1 package (8 ounces) cream cheese,
    softened
1 package (4 ounces) crumbled feta
    cheese, at room temperature
2 tablespoons butter, softened
1 large whole roasted red pepper
8 slices provolone cheese
1 container (6 ounces) prepared basil
    pesto
¼ cup pine nuts or sliced almonds,
    toasted
Basil sprigs, for garnish
Toasted bread slices or crackers, for
    serving

1. In a large bowl, combine cream cheese, feta cheese, and butter. Beat with an electric mixer on high speed until light and fluffy.

2. Line an 8 x 4-inch loaf pan with plastic wrap. Arrange enough red pepper on the bottom of the pan to cover it, trimming to fit. Arrange 6 slices of provolone on top of the pepper and up the sides of the pan. Spoon half the cream cheese mixture over the provolone. Layer ¼ cup pesto over the cheese mixture and sprinkle with all the nuts. Repeat layering with cream cheese and pesto. Top with remaining 2 slices of provolone. Fold in cheese slices on the sides and ends over the pesto. Cover and chill for 8 hours.

3. To serve, invert mold onto serving plate. Peel off the plastic wrap. Garnish with basil sprigs. Cut into slices with a sharp knife and serve with toasted bread or crackers.

Seafood Mousse Ring

Thinly sliced smoked salmon is wrapped around a tuna mousse for a "Tah-dah!" party dish.

PREP TIME: 30 MINUTES • MAKES: 10 TO 12 SERVINGS

10 tablespoons unsalted butter

1 can (10 ounces) white tuna in water, drained

2 tablespoons lemon juice

Pinch white pepper

2 tablespoons chopped fresh dill

1 cup mayonnaise

1 tablespoon capers, drained

1 package (8 ounces) sliced smoked salmon

1 package crisp rye crackers or party pumpernickel bread

Sliced lemons, for garnish

1. In the bowl of a food processor with the steel blade attached, pulse the butter. Add tuna, lemon juice, pepper, and dill. Process until smooth. Stir in mayonnaise and capers.

2. Line a 6-cup ring mold with plastic wrap. Arrange smoked salmon along the sides and bottom of the mold. Spoon in the tuna mixture. Fold remaining salmon over the tuna. Cover with plastic wrap. Refrigerate overnight.

3. To serve, invert the mold onto a serving plate. Peel off plastic wrap. Garnish with lemon slices. Serve with party pumpernickel bread or rye crackers.

Seafood Salad

This is a very forgiving recipe– any combination of similar-flavored shellfish will work. The recipe can be doubled easily.

PREP TIME: 15 MINUTES • MAKES: 8 SERVINGS

2 cups cooked mixed seafood, such
    as shrimp, crabmeat, scallops,
    mussels, cut-up lobster meat
⅔ cup mayonnaise
2 teaspoons grated lime zest
2 tablespoons fresh lime juice
Lime wedges, for garnish

1. In a large bowl, combine the seafood. In a medium bowl, stir together the mayonnaise, lime zest, and lime juice until well mixed. (Can be made ahead. Cover each bowl and refrigerate up to 6 hours.)

2. To serve, add the seafood to the mayonnaise mixture and toss. To serve as a first course for a dinner party, spoon into small serving bowls and garnish each serving with lime wedges. For a buffet, spoon into 3-ounce flat-bottom paper cups and serve in a large bowl filled with crushed ice. Garnish rim of serving bowl with lime wedges.

Blushing Herring Salad

The "blush" comes from the addition of cranberry sauce to the sour cream.

PREP TIME: 15 MINUTES PLUS MARINATING • **MAKES: 16 TO 18 SERVINGS**

2 jars (8 ounces each) refrigerated
   herring in wine sauce
1 cup sour cream
1 can (8 ounces) whole-berry
   cranberry sauce
½ large sweet onion, thinly sliced
1 Granny Smith apple, cored, peeled,
   and chopped
1 loaf (16 ounces) party rye bread

Drain the herring. Cut into bite-sized pieces. Place in a medium bowl. Add remaining ingredients, except the bread, and stir to combine. Cover and refrigerate at least 4 or up to 24 hours. Serve with rye bread.

Gravlax

Thinly sliced and served with a mustard sauce, this cured salmon will be a big hit.

PREP TIME: **10 MINUTES** • MAKES: **8 SERVINGS**

1 ½ teaspoons dry mustard
1 tablespoon gin
1 cup mayonnaise
¼ cup chopped fresh dill
2 tablespoons Dijon mustard
1 tablespoon fresh lemon juice
2 packages (8 ounces each) sliced
    gravlax
Fresh dill sprigs, for garnish
1 loaf pumpernickel bread, cut into
    triangles and lightly toasted

1. In a small bowl, combine mustard and gin; stir. Let stand 30 minutes. Stir in the mayonnaise, chopped dill, Dijon mustard, and lemon juice. Pour into a sauceboat and reserve.

2. Scrape off any spices and dill on the salmon. Arrange slices on a serving platter and garnish with fresh dill sprigs. Serve with mustard sauce and toasted pumpernickel triangles.

Beggars' Purses

The tying with the green onion can take a little practice, so it's best to have a few extra onions just in case.

PREP TIME: 15 MINUTES • MAKES: 20

1 cup sour cream
2 tablespoons minced shallots
2 tablespoons chopped fresh dill
1 teaspoon grated lemon zest
Dash freshly ground pepper
1 bunch green onions
1 package (8 ounces) sliced smoked
　　salmon
2 packages (4.5 ounces each) crepes
　　(found in the produce section of
　　the supermarket)

1. In a small bowl, combine the sour cream, shallots, dill, lemon zest, and pepper. (Can be made ahead, covered, and refrigerated up to 6 hours.)

2. Trim the green tops off the onions (reserve white parts for another use). Slice each piece in half lengthwise. Place on paper towels. Microwave on low power for 20 seconds. Set aside.

3. Just before serving, place a 3-inch piece of salmon in the center of a crepe. Top with a heaping teaspoon of sour cream sauce on salmon. Pull the edges of the crepe up to form a pouch and tie with a green onion. Repeat process using the remainder of the salmon, sour cream, and crepes. Serve immediately.

Scallops in Cream

Use the smaller bay scallops; they are the perfect size for party food. If you can't find the bay scallops, use sea scallops and quarter them.

PREP/COOK TIME: 15 MINUTES • MAKES: 6 TO 8 SERVINGS

1 pound bay scallops
¼ teaspoon salt
Dash white pepper
½ cup Scotch whisky
1 cup heavy cream
1 tablespoon chopped fresh parsley
Dash paprika

1. In a large skillet, combine the scallops, salt, pepper, and Scotch. Cook over high heat for 2 to 3 minutes. Remove scallops with a slotted spoon to a bowl. Reduce the liquid in the skillet by two thirds, stirring frequently. Add any reserved liquid from the scallops to the skillet.

2. Stir in cream and continue reducing to ¾ cup. Remove from heat and stir in the scallops. Sprinkle with parsley and paprika. Serve immediately.

Sole-Orange Seviche

The seafood is marinated in lime juice and the action of the citrus "cooks" or firms the fish. It is important to use only the freshest of fish.

PREP TIME: 20 MINUTES PLUS MARINATING • MAKES: 8 SERVINGS

½ pound sole or red snapper fillets
¾ cup fresh lime juice
½ cup prepared salsa
1 navel orange, peeled and sectioned
½ cup diced fresh avocado
2 tablespoons chopped fresh cilantro
1 tablespoon olive oil
Tortilla chips

1. Cut the fish into ¼-inch cubes. Place in a small bowl and cover with the lime juice. Cover and refrigerate for 5 hours, stirring occasionally, until the fish is opaque and cooked through.

2. In a medium bowl, combine the remaining ingredients except avocado and tortilla chips. Drain the fish; discard lime juice. Rinse fish and pat dry. Add fish to the salsa mixture and stir to combine. Add avocado and stir gently. Serve with tortilla chips.

VARIATION

Scallop-Orange Seviche
Substitute ½ pound sea scallops, cut into ¼-inch cubes, for the sole fillets.

Scallop Canapés

These are another classic appetizer that will never go out of style.

PREP TIME: 45 MINUTES • **BROIL TIME: 5 MINUTES** • **MAKES: 60 PIECES**

15 slices white sandwich bread (from a 16-ounce package)
1 tablespoon butter
⅓ cup minced onion
⅔ cup mayonnaise
¾ cup shredded Swiss cheese
1 tablespoon chopped fresh dill
½ pound raw bay scallops

1. Heat oven to 350°F. With a 1¼-inch round cookie cutter, cut out 4 circles in each bread slice; arrange on a baking sheet. Toast bread for 5 minutes. Turn bread over and continue toasting for 3 more minutes.

2. In a small skillet, melt butter; add onion and cook until soft, about 3 minutes. In a medium bowl, combine onion with the remaining ingredients and stir until well mixed. (Can be made ahead, covered, and refrigerated up to 24 hours.)

3. Heat broiler. Top each of the toasts with a tablespoon of the scallop mixture. Broil until scallops are cooked through, 5 minutes. Serve warm.

VARIATIONS

Crab Canapés
Substitute ½ pound crabmeat. (The crab version cannot be made ahead.)

Shrimp Canapés
Substitute ½ pound frozen shelled and deveined shrimp, thawed and tails removed. Finely chop the shrimp. Add ¼ teaspoon bottled jalapeño sauce.

Smoked Trout on Endive

Smoked fish can be found in supermarket deli sections. If you can't find trout, substitute other smoked fish, such as mackerel or whitefish.

PREP TIME: 20 MINUTES • MAKES: 18 TO 20

1 smoked trout fillet, skinned (about
   5 ounces)
⅓ cup sour cream
1 tablespoon chopped chives
2 large heads Belgian endive

1. Remove bones from the trout. Break fish into small pieces and place in a bowl. Break up with a fork.

2. Add sour cream and chives and mix into a paste.

3. Separate the leaves of the endive. Spoon a teaspoonful of trout mixture at the stem end of the leaf. Continue making more with the remaining trout mixture and endive leaves.

VARIATION

Garlic Cheese on Endive
Combine ¼ cup garlic cheese, ¼ cup sour cream, and 1 tablespoon chopped chives until well mixed. Spoon onto the end of the endive leaf.

Steamed Mussels

For a casual party, place a large pot of steamed mussels within easy reach and let everyone scoop out their portion into small bowls.

PREP TIME: 20 MINUTES • **COOK TIME: 5 MINUTES** • **MAKES: 16**

1 can (13.75 ounces) chicken broth
½ cup white wine
3 tablespoons chopped garlic
1 cup heavy cream
3 pounds fresh mussels, scrubbed
¼ cup chopped fresh parsley

1. In a large saucepot over medium-high heat, combine chicken broth, wine, and garlic. Heat to a boil and boil for 10 minutes. Pour in the heavy cream and continue cooking until reduced by a fourth.

2. Meanwhile, scrub the mussels well. Add mussels to the boiling liquid in the saucepot, cover, and cook for 5 minutes or until mussels have opened. (Discard any unopened shells.) Sprinkle with parsley. Serve immediately.

Wasabi Tuna Bites

For a first-course presentation, cut the tuna into larger pieces and serve the crackers and sauce on the side.

PREP TIME: 10 MINUTES • BAKE TIME: 5 MINUTES • MAKES: 8 TO 10 SERVINGS

1 pound fresh tuna steak
½ cup plus 2 teaspoons soy sauce
1 tablespoon plus ½ teaspoon wasabi
   powder
1 tablespoon vegetable oil
2 teaspoons chopped garlic
⅓ cup mayonnaise
1 package rice crackers
Fresh cilantro, for garnish

1. Cut the tuna into 1-inch pieces. In a glass baking dish, combine ½ cup soy sauce, 1 tablespoon wasabi powder, oil and garlic; add tuna and toss to coat. Cover and refrigerate for 30 minutes.

2. Heat oven to 450°F. Drain the tuna; discard marinade. Place tuna on a lightly greased baking sheet. Bake for 5 minutes.

3. In a small bowl, combine mayonnaise, 2 teaspoons soy sauce, and ½ teaspoon wasabi powder; stir.

4. Place a piece of tuna on each rice cracker and top with a dab of sauce. Garnish each one with a cilantro leaf and serve immediately.

Curried Steamed Mussels

The coconut milk used in this recipe is unsweetened and can be found in the Asian section of the supermarket.

PREP TIME: 20 MINUTES • **COOK TIME: 5 MINUTES** • **MAKES: 16**

2 tablespoons olive oil

½ cup chopped onion

½ cup chopped fresh red bell pepper

1 can (13.5 ounces) unsweetened coconut milk

2 tablespoons bottled mild curry paste

3 pounds fresh mussels, scrubbed

⅓ cup chopped sweet basil

1 tablespoon fresh lime juice

1. In a large saucepot, heat the oil. Add onion and pepper and cook for 2 minutes, stirring occasionally. Stir in the coconut milk and curry paste; cover and cook for 5 minutes over medium heat.

2. Increase the heat to high. Add the mussels; cover and cook for 5 minutes or until mussels have opened. (Discard any unopened shells.) Stir in the basil and lime juice. Serve immediately.

VARIATION

Curried Shrimp
Prepare curry sauce as directed above. Substitute 2 pounds frozen large cooked, shelled, and deveined shrimp for the mussels. Cover and cook for 3 minutes, until shrimp thaw.

Oysters Rockefeller

Ask the fishmonger to shuck the oysters for you and give you the shells and the oyster meat in separate containers—I do not recommend learning how to open oysters the day of the party.

PREP TIME: 15 MINUTES • **BAKE TIME: 10 MINUTES** • **MAKES: 24**

1 package (10 ounces) frozen chopped spinach, cooked according to package directions

1 stick (½ cup) butter, melted and divided

1 tablespoon fresh lemon juice

1 tablespoon anise-flavored liqueur

½ teaspoon hot salt

24 shucked oysters, shells reserved

⅓ cup plain dried bread crumbs

6 slices precooked bacon, crumbled

1. Heat oven to 475°F. Drain the cooked spinach and squeeze well. In medium bowl, combine spinach with 5 tablespoons melted butter, lemon juice, liqueur, and hot salt; toss until well mixed. (Can be made ahead, covered, and set aside at room temperature up to 4 hours.)

2. Arrange 24 of the oyster shells on two baking sheets. Place an oyster in each shell. Spoon the spinach mixture evenly over each oyster, about 1 tablespoon per shell. Add bread crumbs to remaining 3 tablespoons melted butter and sprinkle the crumbs over each oyster. Top with the crumbled bacon. Bake for 10 minutes. Serve immediately.

Broiled Tequila Shrimp

Use two bamboo skewers for each batch of shrimp instead of one—they're much easier to flip during cooking.

PREP TIME: 1 HOUR 10 MINUTES • **BROIL TIME: 5 MINUTES** • **MAKES: 8 SERVINGS**

2 pounds large frozen shelled and
   deveined shrimp, thawed
¼ cup fresh lime juice
¼ cup tequila
1 tablespoon olive oil
1 jalapeño chile, minced
½ teaspoon salt
Bamboo skewers
1½ cups prepared salsa

1. In a medium bowl, combine shrimp, lime juice, tequila, oil, jalapeño, and salt; toss to coat shrimp. Refrigerate 1 hour, stirring occasionally.

2. Thread 3 or 4 shrimp onto two skewers, depending on the length of bamboo; repeat threading remaining shrimp. Heat broiler (or grill). Broil 4 inches from heat source for 2 or 3 minutes per side. Serve with salsa.

Pâté en Croûte

This could also be called Foie Gras Wellington. Serve with Dijon mustard and the French mini sour pickles called cornichons.

PREP TIME: 10 MINUTES • BAKE TIME: 20 MINUTES • MAKES: 18 TO 20 SLICES

1 sheet thawed puff pastry (from a
    17.2-ounce package)
1 package (7 ounces) truffle mousse
    (liver pâté), trimmed of gelatin
1 egg yolk, mixed with 2 teaspoons
    water

1. Heat oven to 425°F. Unfold one sheet of puff pastry on a lightly floured surface. Cut pastry in half lengthwise. Roll out each half to a 10 x 12-inch rectangle.

2. Cut the pâté to fit the length of the pastry, but not wider than 3 inches. Divide pâté between two sheets and wrap pastry up and over, enrobing the pâté. Brush all sides of the pastry with the egg mixture. Press ends to seal. Place, seam-side down, on a lightly oiled baking sheet. Brush top of pastry with egg mixture.

3. Bake the rolls until pastry is lightly browned, about 20 minutes. Remove from oven, wrap immediately in foil, and roll into a tight log. Refrigerate overnight. To serve, let wrapped rolls stand at room temperature 30 minutes. Unwrap and cut into ¼-inch slices.

VARIATION

Pâté de Campagne en Croûte
Substitute country-style (coarse-textured) pâté for the smooth mousse. Use the same amount.

Blue Cheese with Pears

This can be made with any of the three major blue cheeses: Gorgonzola, Stilton, or Roquefort, or a combination. Serve with unpeeled red pears for a lovely presentation.

PREP TIME: 15 MINUTES • MAKES: 12 TO 16 SERVINGS

11 ounces cream cheese, softened (an 8-ounce plus a 3-ounce package)
½ cup unsalted butter, softened
8 ounces Gorgonzola, Roquefort, or Stilton cheese
½ cup chopped walnuts, toasted
4 pears

1. In a large bowl, combine the cream cheese, butter, and blue cheese. Beat with an electric mixer on low speed until well mixed and smooth.

2. Line an 8-inch pie plate with plastic wrap. Spoon cheese mixture into the prepared pie plate. Cover and refrigerate up to 3 hours or until firm.

3. To serve, invert cheese mixture onto large serving plate and remove plastic wrap. Garnish the top with nuts. Slice the pears and arrange around the cheese.

Prosciutto-Wrapped Melon

This is a perfect addition to a prepared antipasto platter.

PREP TIME: 10 MINUTES • MAKES: ABOUT 24

1 small cantaloupe, seeded
2 packages (4 ounces each) thinly
   sliced prosciutto
Lime wedges

Cut the melon into 1-inch wedges
and remove the rind. Wrap each wedge
with a slice of prosciutto. Arrange on a
serving plate and garnish with lime
wedges. Serve immediately.

VARIATIONS

Prosciutto-Wrapped Asparagus
Substitute 24 spears of asparagus for
the melon. Cut the prosciutto slices in
half, crosswise. Cut the woody ends from
the asapragus spears and then cut each
spear into two 4-inch pieces. Steam just
until bright green. Dunk aparagus in cold
water to stop cooking. Drain, pat dry with
a paper towel, and wrap each with a piece
of prosciutto.

Prosciutto-Wrapped Pears
Substitute 3 ripe Comice pears, each cut
into 12 wedges, for the melon. Cut the
prosciutto in half, crosswise, as above.

Chocolate-Hazelnut Tartlets

No party is complete without some sort of sweet. These fit the bill nicely.

PREP TIME: **10 MINUTES** • BAKE TIME: **5 MINUTES** • MAKES: **30**

2 packages (2.1 ounces each) mini phyllo dough tart shells
1 jar (13 ounces) chocolate hazelnut spread
2 tablespoons heavy cream
2 ounces semisweet chocolate, finely chopped
Whole hazelnuts, for garnish

1. Heat oven to 450°F. Place dough shells on a baking sheet and bake 5 minutes to crisp. Cool completely.

2. Spoon a tablespoon of chocolate hazelnut spread into each tart shell.

3. Place cream and chocolate in a small microwaveproof bowl. Microwave at 50% power for 1 minute. Stir. Continue heating in 15-second increments until chocolate is melted and smooth. Spoon melted chocolate on top of chocolate hazelnut spread and top each with a whole hazelnut. Refrigerate until chocolate is set. (Can be made ahead, covered, and refrigerated up to 3 days.)

Lemon Clouds

An elegant ending. At cocktail parties, where appetizers substitute for dinner, it's fun to finish on a sweet note.

PREP TIME: 10 MINUTES • BAKE TIME: 5 MINUTES • MAKES: 30

2 packages (2.1 ounces each) mini
    phyllo dough tart shells
½ cup heavy cream
2 tablespoons confectioners' sugar
⅓ cup lemon curd
30 fresh raspberries or blueberries

1. Heat oven to 450°F. Place dough shells on a baking sheet and bake 5 minutes to crisp. Cool completely.

2. In a medium bowl, whip cream and sugar until soft peaks form. Gently fold in lemon curd.

3. Spoon cream mixture into tart shells. Refrigerate. (Can be made ahead, covered, and refrigerated up to 2 days.) Just before serving, top each tartlet with a berry.